COME | *unto* | ME

COME | *unto* | ME

God's call
to intimacy

JAMES P. GILLS, M.D.

CREATION
HOUSE PRESS

COME UNTO ME: GOD'S CALL TO INTIMACY
by James P. Gills, M.D.
Published by Creation House Press
A part of Strang Communications Company
600 Rinehart Road
Lake Mary, Florida 32746
www.creationhouse.com

Unless otherwise noted, all Scripture quotations are from the New King James Version of the Bible. Copyright © 1979, 1980, 1982 by Thomas Nelson, Inc., publishers. Used by permission.

Scripture quotations marked AMP are from the Amplified Bible. Old Testament copyright © 1965, 1987 by the Zondervan Corporation. The Amplified New Testament copyright © 1954, 1958, 1987 by the Lockman Foundation. Used by permission.

Scripture quotations marked NAS are from the New American Standard Bible. Copyright © 1960, 1962, 1963, 1968, 1971, 1972, 1973, 1975, 1977 by the Lockman Foundation. Used by permission. (www.Lockman.org)

Cover design by Judith McKittrick
Interior design by David Bilby

Library of Congress Control Number: 2003101122
International Standard Book Number: 1-59185-214-5

03 04 05 06   8 7 6 5 4 3 2 1
Printed in the United States of America

Dedicated to some very special people...

St. Luke's patients.

I love you all.

JAMES P. GILLS, M.D.

CONTENTS

CHAPTER 1

By Divine Appointment

Mt. Sinai. Not just another mountain, but *the* mountain—the meeting place of God and man. Silent. Majestic. Soundless echoes cutting a swath across the ages. Gebal Musa (mountain of Moses) stood a mute witness to the glory of God and to the relentless cry of His heart for a people who would be wholly His.

I heard the call from the mountain…"Come unto Me, and I will be a Father to you. Come unto Me, and I will save and deliver you from all your enemies. Come unto Me, and learn of Me. I will teach you. Abide in Me, and I will give you rest. Take joy in Me. Rejoice in My presence, for I, the Lord your Maker, will be your Husband, and you will be My Bride. Come unto Me."

Many believe that here on this mountain—on these very slopes—Moses climbed, drawn inexorably by the summons of God. Drawn away from the mundane task of tending sheep, he determined to discover the secret of a bush that burned without being consumed. Find the truth he did—and with its finding was forever changed.

Centuries later, pursuing my own desire to discover the spiritual significance of this land, I stood at the foot of Mount Sinai. Sensing in the predawn silence the breath of antiquity descending from the heights, I recalled the Bible stories associated with this mountain: the burning bush, the Ten Commandments and the giving of the Law. With a feeling of awe and reverence, I stood gazing at the peak of Gebal Musa. I could almost hear the faint, rumbling echoes of eons-old thunder reverberating through the corridor of time.

Never have I seen a mountain peak that I did not want to climb. But *this* mountain, so alike, yet unlike, any other, was touched by the hand of the Living God! I wanted desperately to climb it, to become a part of it. Now that the long-awaited moment had finally arrived, I was overwhelmed. Struck with the immensity of this ancient land, desert stretching endlessly behind me while the mountain loomed directly ahead, I felt in danger of being swallowed alive. But I came to climb, and climb I would, for I too was in search of an answer.

Beginning the ascent as one of Jamie Buckingham's group of twelve desert voyagers, I could contain myself no longer. Solitude would be a welcome companion. Needing to pray, and filled with an urge to run and jog up the mountain, I broke away from the others. If I could only seek God and ask Him to reveal the significance of the Sinai…What subtle truth, what life-changing revelation, what priceless pearl lay patiently waiting to be discovered amid this sea of sand and rock?

Nearing the summit, my heart pounded rhythmically while my lungs fitfully labored to breathe in the cool, dry, thin air of the desert's higher elevation. Again and again I tasted of that inner hunger for answers, that yearning to be near God, to be one with Him. Suddenly, as the sun began rising like a giant golden bubble from the cauldron of the desert floor, I was alone atop Mt. Sinai.

In the stillness of the morning my spirit was anything but quiet. I found an isolated rock, sat down and began reading my Bible, seeking that hidden pearl. My troubled mind wanted only to know the truths calling to me ever so softly just beyond the range of hearing. But the written truth from the Scriptures I read fell off my brain "like water from a duck's back." One after another they passed uneventfully before my eyes until my searching gaze finally focused upon the words of Exodus 19:4, "*I . . . brought you to Myself.*"

There it was. In that special way God's Spirit has of opening a previously locked door and imparting fresh revelation, I knew Jehovah God was making a statement to His people, including me, from this rock called Sinai. It was not the fire and thunder He was declaring. Neither was it the parting of the Red Sea, the giving of the Law, the Ten Commandments or even the stone tablets on which they were written. It was none of these, yet it was all of them. God's deepest desire from His heart of love cried for intimacy with man.

Hundreds of times before I had read the words, "You have seen what I did to the Egyptians, and how I bore you on eagles' wings and brought you to Myself" (Exodus 19:4). Yes, the words I knew, but the underlying meaning continued to escape me. While I was sitting there on the mountain, God was speaking, and this verse came alive with new meaning. My mind was still filled with the same questions, but now I was filled with a calm assurance, and I knew the answers would not remain hidden long.

Why would Almighty God, the omniscient, omnipotent and omnipresent Creator of the universe, want me, a sinner, to be close to Him? The immensity of such love intrigued me endlessly. Is it possible that the call that once sang forth from Mt. Sinai has, like an arrow loosed from the mightiest of bows, already struck the mark and fulfilled its purpose?

Hardly. God's greatest desire, His cry of love—Come unto

Me…Learn of Me…Abide in Me—is still going forth. God has not changed. Intimate, unbroken fellowship with us is our Father's wish as much now as then. He is love (1 John 4:8, 16), and His love never fails (1 Corinthians 13:8). What then? Has man changed so much from the days of the great Exodus? Is our hearing any less acute than the Israelites'? Suddenly, with the coming of this new insight into the Father-heart of God, I saw my life reflected in the words, *"I…brought you."*

My previous attempts to achieve intimacy with God were just that—merely attempts. I was striving to do what God said He would do. My trials, passions, successes and even failures closely paralleled the experiences of Moses and the Israelites.

How often I had cried, "Lord, You alone are my God, and I am Your servant. Use me, I pray, as an instrument of Your love. Glorify Yourself through me." God heard those prayers. He responded to the call of my heart and said, "Come unto Me." So, come I would, but I had not yet learned *to remain* in Him.

I would come to God, throw myself at His feet and say, "Here I am." But I did not know how to abide in His presence, to live in the shadow of the Almighty. The title of a book written by Jill Briscoe—*Here Am I; Send Aaron!*[1]— resembled this aspect of my Christian walk far too closely. I came to God when He called, but often my, "Here I am…" was too quickly followed by, "Send my brother." One day while listening to Vance Havner on the radio, I heard him make a statement that pierced my heart. Vance said, "Your talk…is ahead of your walk." *How true*, I thought.

God called me, as He does all of us, from "burning bushes" placed strategically along familiar pathways. Sometimes the Holy Spirit speaks to us through the "burning bush" of His Word. At other times the bush is represented by fellow

Christians or specific circumstances that He uses to confirm something He has revealed during times of prayer. I failed to respond to some of them; however, I did respond to others. One of these burning bushes to which I did respond was the call to become an eye surgeon.

Using the latest state-of-the-art equipment, medicine and medical techniques, each day I rearrange the eye. Then, in ways not even top scientists understand, God brings healing. He designed and created the human body. Cuts and scratches heal themselves and broken bones knit together again, all without any conscious effort on our part. How illustrative this is of God's concern, of His loving forethought for us.

The Lord is working out a carefully orchestrated plan of love for mankind, a plan that is perfectly in line with His nature. When we hurt, He desires to comfort. When we are wounded, He brings healing. This is a truth revealed from the Sinai. When God calls us to Himself, it is His desire to keep us close, to nurture, feed, comfort and strengthen His children. Sadly, not all will come to Him when He calls. And of those who do come, many will not stay. But those who do remain will learn the secret of resting in His name, of faithfully trusting in God's ability to fulfill all His promises.

The trek of the Israelites from Egypt to the Promised Land of milk and honey teaches much that will help everyone who would successfully respond to the call from the mountain. First of all, God never prefers judgment. The plans that He has for us are plans for good and not evil (Jeremiah 29:11). And He is a just and holy God whose sacrificial love will not be mocked. That is why, although He does not wish to execute judgment, He does make provision for it. Throughout history, judgment always comes as a result of sin, never without cause. This is our God's way—love first.

CHAPTER 2

Out of Bondage

Thousands of years ago in the land of Egypt, while a Pharaoh ruled who knew Joseph, the children of Israel prospered even while they were in captivity. Their numbers increased, and they were looked upon with favor. With the passage of time and a shift in Egyptian leadership, everything changed. Suddenly, the rapidly expanding multitude appeared to be a threat. To keep from being overrun by them, the Egyptians began making slaves of the Israelites.

Day after day, year after year, the people implored God to deliver them. He heard and responded by sending a man—Moses. He was an Israelite who had been raised an Egyptian, a warrior par excellence turned nomadic wanderer, a murderer running from the past and a shepherd guarding the flocks of his father-in-law. God responded to the peoples' anguished plea, but not as they expected.

Drawn by a burning bush to the mountain, Moses responded instantly by saying, "Here I am." Then he received his commission from God. It was there that a relationship began, there that God declared His love:

> And the LORD said: "I have surely seen the oppression of My people who are in Egypt, and have heard their cry because of their taskmasters, for I know their sorrows. So I have come down to deliver them out of the hand of the Egyptians, and to bring them up from that land to a good and large land, to a land flowing with milk and honey...Now therefore, behold, the cry of the children of Israel has come to Me, and I have also seen the oppression with which the Egyptians oppress them. Come now, therefore, and I will send you to Pharaoh that you may bring My people, the children of Israel, out of Egypt."
>
> —EXODUS 3:7–10

Imagine how this must have shocked Moses. Forty years earlier he had made a grave mistake in Egypt. Seeing a fellow Israelite being beaten by an over-zealous taskmaster, and trying to protect the man, Moses killed the Egyptian assailant and buried him in the sand. When the deed was exposed, ironically by some of his own people, he fled to the wilderness where he remained for many years.

Now God was telling him to go back to Egypt. Moses' earlier reply at the burning bush of, "Here I am," now turned to, "Who am I that I should go to Pharaoh...?" (Exodus 3:11).

Where was the once-powerful man who thought he could deliver a nation by the strength of his sword arm? The wilderness years had wrought dramatic changes in Moses. No longer the indomitable warrior, he was older, wiser, more meek and humble. Broken, surrendered and dependent upon the Lord, he knew his weakness. Moses had seen his true nature revealed by the unforgiving desert wasteland and was now just where God wanted him—an empty vessel waiting to be filled.

Almighty God, from whom nothing is hidden, who sees

through all our carefully prepared and diligently maintained facades, waits for us to see ourselves through His eyes. Then, despairing in our weakness, discouraged at the sight of our folly, we hear God call us to Him, and He teaches us the first important lesson:

> The fear of the LORD is the beginning of wisdom,
> And the knowledge of the Holy One is understanding.
> —PROVERBS 9:10

There in the Sinai wilderness, in the presence of Jehovah God, Moses learned this lesson. Standing on holy ground, Moses "hid his face, for he was afraid to look upon God" (Exod. 3:6).

The commission followed next, and Moses replied, in essence, "Lord, not me. I can't speak. I'm not eloquent. Who should I say sent me? Lord, send someone else."

With his response came lesson two.

> I will certainly be with you. And this shall be a sign to you that I have sent you: When you have brought the people out of Egypt, you shall serve God on this mountain.
> —EXODUS 3:12

God did more than send Moses on a mission. He promised to be with him while Moses ventured back into Egypt to bring the people out. God would be with them when Moses and the Israelites returned to this very mountain in Sinai where they would worship God. The Lord promises us, as He did later promise Moses, "My presence will go with you, and I will give you rest" (Exodus 33:14). For Moses, this promised rest came after he petitioned the Lord saying, "Now therefore, I pray, if I have found grace in Your sight, show me now Your way, that I may know You and that I may find grace in Your sight. And consider that this nation is Your people" (Exodus 33:13).

For a lasting relationship to develop, both parties involved must come to know each other intimately. God desired to give His people understanding, true divine understanding, and not the "wisdom" of Egypt. According to Scripture, such understanding is nothing less than knowledge of the Holy One.

Our heavenly Father wants to reveal His loving nature to us. Yes, He knows our every thought and wants us to know Him even as we are known.

Moses obeyed God and went back to Egypt. With Aaron as his spokesman, they marched in to Pharaoh and declared, "Thus says the LORD God of Israel: 'Let My people go, that they may hold a feast to Me in the wilderness'" (Exodus 5:1).

Pharaoh was not impressed; neither was he amused. With disdain he responded, "Who is the LORD, that I should obey His voice to let Israel go? I do not know the LORD, nor will I let Israel go" (Exodus 5:2). Contrary to the immediate, victorious deliverance Moses and Aaron were expecting, Pharaoh gave commands to make it even more difficult for the Israelites. Why didn't Pharaoh have any desire to do what God said? Because he did not *know* Him—he even admitted it. The day would come when Pharaoh surely would know who God was.

But in the meantime, by hardening Pharaoh's heart for a season, the Lord made way for even a greater purpose to be fulfilled, one His people did not yet see: "that I may show these signs of Mine before him" (Exodus 10:1).

The Israelites needed more than just to escape from Egypt. Being released from the land of bondage without complete freedom from its authority would serve no purpose.

To live in a state of fear, continually looking over their shoulders to see if the enemy was catching up, was not God's way. So the oppression increased. The situation, once difficult, became impossible, and the people complained even more.

As the apostle John tells us, our God is love. Like the Israelites, when we pray for release from difficult situations and the difficulties multiply, we too cry, "Where are You, Lord? If you love me so much, how could You let this happen? Why don't You answer?" When we are in the midst of trouble, questions seem overwhelming. We, like the children of Israel, tend to expect God to conform to *our* image of love. This is where the confusion begins.

We must understand the meaning of *agape love*. Godly love. No man or woman is born with such love. Since the Fall of Adam and Eve, it has not existed in human nature. It comes only from God. He alone knows our every desire and promises to supply our every requirement. Agape love—true charity—is a totally selfless giving in a desire to supply whatever is needed. Sometimes our desire to give coincides with another's needs. Usually it does not.

Often this is difficult for us to understand. It was true for the Israelites, and it is true today, especially if we are the ones being oppressed or persecuted. The fault lies not with God, however. Our understanding of Him is sadly deficient. The Holy One is still calling. He longs for us to learn of Him, to rest content, knowing that He is working a far greater purpose in us than the circumstances in which we find ourselves.

Jesus Christ, the promised Messiah, also caused great consternation among the learned Jews of His day. Like Moses, He was not the deliverer they had been expecting. The lack of an intimate relationship with the God they studied caused them to reject His ultimate love. They had prayed for a Messiah to deliver them from Roman oppression. In the fullness of time God sent His own Son to release His people from a far greater bondage, the bondage of sin and eternal death.

After Moses endured many rejections from Pharaoh, the time was finally right for the Israelites' deliverance. On the night before the great exodus from Egypt, God gave specific instructions that were to be obeyed explicitly. The Passover was at hand. God's judgment was about to be seen. For protection, the Israelites were to sacrifice a lamb, a spotless and unblemished lamb. Its blood was to be applied to the doorposts of their homes, and then, before morning, the animal was to be eaten. Only in this way would they be protected from the judgment that was about to befall Egypt.

> For I will pass through the land of Egypt on that night, and will strike all the firstborn in the land of Egypt, both man and beast; and against all the gods of Egypt I will execute judgment: I am the LORD.
> —EXODUS 12:12–13

With a single stroke God destroyed the strength and hope of Egypt, and the stage was set for the next step. After the Israelites left Pharaoh's country, he recovered somewhat from the shock. Enraged, he gathered his armies and set out to slaughter the children of Israel. But God had other plans. Never again would the Pharaoh, who symbolized the authority and power of Satan and his system, have dominion over the people of God. Deliverance was assured, but it would not be by the strength of an army or its weapons.

Led by the pillar of fire by night and the pillar of cloud by day, the Israelites arrived at the borders of the Red Sea. The Egyptians in all their fury followed close behind. Seemingly trapped, they despaired. There was no escape, at least none that their human understanding could detect. Jehovah wanted His people to know that He was far greater than any obstacles they could encounter. He wanted their trust, their unqualified love.

> And Moses said to the people, "Do not be afraid. Stand still, and see the salvation of the LORD, which He will accomplish for you today. For the Egyptians whom you see today, you shall see again no more forever."
> —EXODUS 14:13

And so it was. As God directed, Moses stretched the rod of God over the waters. A strong east wind began blowing, and the water parted. With shimmering walls of water on either side of them, the children of Israel crossed over the Red Sea on dry ground. Once safely across, they watched as God fulfilled His Word. The walls of water collapsed, and Pharaoh's pursuing army was no more.

At last, after four hundred years of bondage, the Israelites were free. How greatly they praised God! It was known throughout the world that the God of the Hebrews was a mighty God who showed Himself strong on behalf of His people. He judged evil in the land, destroyed its authority and set His people free to begin a brand-new life.

At one point during my own modern-day wilderness journey, I was running alongside the Egyptian International Highway. As I ran, I began contemplating the significance of the Red Sea crossing, the grand event that had marked a turning point for the Israelites.

As a Christian I looked at those earlier historic events and saw how they foreshadowed a greater salvation and turning point in God's relationship with man. The Passover, the sacrificial lamb, the covering of protection because of its blood, the death of Pharaoh, the Red Sea—all pointed to the greatest sacrifice and deliverance this world would ever know. Jesus Christ, the Messiah of Israel, the Lamb and Savior would, through His own blood, forever protect mankind from God's judgment upon sin. The Passover stands as a symbol of Christ's sacrifice. It was, in fact, during the celebration of the Passover feast that Jesus was crucified. He conquered death and, in so doing, destroyed the authority of Satan.

We need only to respond to the call of the Father and to accept the sacrifice of the Lamb of God. The Jews of Jesus' day could not believe the idea that through an ultimate act of agape love, God gave what was needed to restore man to a place of fellowship with Him. He wanted a relationship, so He gave Himself.

All did not end with the payment of sin on the cross, any more than did the Israelites' journey end with their escape from Egypt. They crossed the Red Sea. Jesus rose from the dead! Each represents a transformation, a new way of living, a complete separation from the past and all it stands for.

Paul the Apostle wrote to the Roman believers:

> Therefore we were buried with Him through baptism into death, that just as Christ was raised from the dead by the glory of the Father, even so we also should walk in newness of life…For he who has died has been freed from sin.
>
> —ROMANS 6:4, 7

In another letter to the church at Colossae he speaks again of a "death" to the old way of life:

> …having been buried with Him in baptism, in which you were also raised up with Him through faith in the working of God, who raised Him from the dead. And when you were dead in your transgressions and the

uncircumcision of your flesh, He made you alive
together with Him, having forgiven us all our trans-
gressions, having canceled out the certificate of debt
consisting of decrees against us and which was hostile
to us; and He has taken it out of the way, having
nailed it to the cross. When He had disarmed the
rulers and authorities, He made a public display of
them, having triumphed over them through Him.
—COLOSSIANS 2:12–15

So essential is the principle of complete separation from
the bondage of sin, that the phrase, "baptism in Christ," is
mentioned 164 times in the Bible! The call from the Sinai
at the Red Sea, then, is a call to a new way of life through
death of the old nature. We are free from the power of sin
the moment we accept Jesus as Lord and Savior. No longer
is Satan our master. Though he will surely tempt us to sin,
his power is broken. Through the broken body of our Lord,
His shed blood, the stripes He bore, His death and glorious
resurrection, we are free!

Every time the body of Christ gathers at the communion
table it is to remember the sacrificial death of Jesus, the
Lamb of God. An enigma to the Jewish leaders of His day,
Love conquered. God executed judgment upon every man
and beast of Egypt, and against all the gods of that land. Jesus
told His disciples, "Now is the judgment of this world; now
the ruler of this world will be cast out" (John 12:31).

With the "crossing of the Red Sea" a new life begins. Our
complete salvation—baptism into Christ, sanctification and
call to holiness—prepares us to receive the gift of God—
power from on high. This new life cannot be lived after the
fashion of the old, and it is beyond our ability to perform.
The Father has supplied the answer.

Before His death, Jesus told the disciples:

> If you love Me, keep My commandments. And I will pray the Father, and He will give you another Helper, that He may abide with you forever.
>
> —JOHN 14:15–16

After His resurrection, in His last words to His followers before ascending into heaven, Jesus reminded His followers of the coming of the Holy Spirit.

> But you shall receive power when the Holy Spirit has come upon you; and you shall be witnesses to Me in Jerusalem, and in all Judea and Samaria, and to the end of the earth.
>
> —ACTS 1:8

Leaving the bondage of our spiritual Egypt buried behind, we are to go forth victoriously in the power of the Spirit to follow a brand-new path—the way that leads to the mountain and on to the promised land.

CHAPTER 3

Learning a New Walk

At the age of fourteen, I began my walk to the mountain. That was the year of my own "Red Sea crossing," or salvation experience. The initial surge of belief did not manifest itself as great faith immediately. Much time—years—would elapse, and still there was a disconcerting lack of consistency in this area on my part.

As a Sunday school teacher at eighteen, I knew *about* God and tried to stay in communion with the God of my perception, but I failed. I did not really know Him and I could not possibly understand Him. We may read or hear about someone, and even learn the things that please him. But unless we understand and know that person's heart we will not know why he is pleased. God does not want us to serve Him in ignorance; His desire is that we know His heart of love.

In my quest to know God I was operating from a misconception about the nature of true love. I knew little, if anything, of the selfless, sacrificial quality of agape love. How could I? Without experiencing God's heart of compassion it simply was not possible. To me, love was something earned by obedience; compassion I saw as weakness. So I tried to earn God's love.

As a young adult, I embraced a certain image of how a male was to perform in society. Thinking "love" was seen as something weak, sissified, indecisive and ineffectual, I tried to conform to the "macho" image. Looking back I see how silly, how futile, all this really was. Pride, envy, greed, spiritual laziness and lust gave evidence of a "self" that was still very much alive.

I soon discovered that lifting weights to develop masculinity, owning a Porsche to signify my "having arrived," or even marrying a very beautiful woman brought no lasting measure of peace to my life. My relationship with God was not all it could be. Although He still reigned on His throne in the heavenlies, in my heart I had enthroned a subtle competitor—self. At thirty-four years of age I faced the realization that there was nothing in life onto which I could hold but Jesus. He alone is our solid rock, our sure foundation.

The pressure of a large medical practice, political and otherwise, was more than I could handle. A lack of family understanding and support served to heighten these feelings. All the things—externals upon which I depended to sustain me—suddenly seemed like sandcastles in the face of an incoming tide. There loomed the ever-present danger of it all being swept away in a moment's notice. Reading God's Word helped. Praying did too, but it was like prescribing aspirin for a swollen appendix. Surgery was required.

I was facing another "burning bush," another opportunity to choose. God was calling me to take one more step on the journey to Canaan. Before the promised land, a meeting on the mountain awaited me.

A committed spiritual life cannot be obtained; it is learned. Moving from a mere belief in God's omnipotence to a vital, living relationship with the omnipotent God is not without difficulty. The Lord Jesus Himself tells us to deny ourselves, pick up our cross daily and follow Him (Luke 9:23). We cannot come to God on our own terms whenever the whim takes us. God calls us to this trek, long and arduous though it may be, because it is during the journey that He prepares us for the meeting on the mountain. God reveals Himself to the heart responding to His call.

In each of our lives there will be times when we come to "bitter waters." They usually appear when things seem to be going along rather drearily, and we are looking for that something to save the day for us. Suddenly, there appears a beautiful package, wrapped up neatly and adorned with a fancy bow on top. We excitedly rush to unwrap it. Pulling the paper off, though, we uncover a disappointment waiting to happen.

The world would have us drink deeply of these bitter cups and just "keep on keepin' on." This law of the jungle mentality (survival of the fittest) teaches that we must fight through, conquering every foe by our innate abilities and taking the bitter with the sweet. Or we go to the opposite extreme and try to avoid every trace of frustration and suffering. We have all heard of the expression, "If it feels good, do it." Certainly this is not God's way, either.

After crossing the Red Sea the children of Israel entered the Wilderness of Shur. For three long days they journeyed, while overhead the desert sun glared, baking the moisture from their bodies. Finally, mouths parched and bodies weak from the sweltering heat, they came to a clear pool of sparkling water. Imagine their cries of dismay as, stooping to drink, they discovered the water was too bitter!

To the natural mind, a mind grown accustomed to the ways of Egypt, this appears cruel and unjust. Delivered from oppression only to die of exposure and dehydration? Our God is not cruel. In His love He was preparing to unveil a truth that goes far deeper than the supplying of bodily needs.

19

He was offering the Israelites, and every child to come, a glimpse through the desert to His heart of love.

Complaining, just as any child who suddenly thinks himself betrayed would complain, the people cried out against Moses. He, in turn, cried out to God "…and the LORD showed him a tree. When he cast it into the waters, the waters were made sweet" (Exodus 15:25).

A tree. Perhaps they were expecting something as dramatic as the parting of the sea. If so, they were sorely disappointed. Moses' simple act of obedience—throwing a specific tree into the bitter waters—was all that was needed. Instantly bitterness gave way to sweetness. God was teaching trust to His children. He wanted them to understand that, whether or not a miracle was in progress, they were being kept by the same power that delivered them from the Egyptian army. He is doing the same for His children today.

The tree symbolizes the agent of God's delivering power, and was the instrument through which this power was released at Marah. There are no impossibilities with God, just further opportunities for the bitter to become sweet. The tree foreshadowed the cross of Jesus Christ.

We read that on the cross Jesus openly destroyed Satan's authority. Yet, when we are faced with the appearance of this toothless lion, we often lose our composure. When trouble comes our way we may even throw the tree into the midst of our troubled waters—*apply the cross* to the situation—but deliverance and peace are often slow in coming. Like the Israelites, we are guilty of overlooking one simple truth: The cross is not to be *applied*; it is to be *experienced*!

We do not need to learn to *run* to the cross when crisis comes; we need to learn to *abide* there continually. It is in the shelter of the cross that we become the righteousness of God in Him (2 Corinthians 5:21). Divinity and humanity meet where the blood of the Lamb flows, where the Vine was wounded that we might be grafted in (John 15). His life, His power, His Spirit flow into us in direct proportion to our experience of this union. As it deepens, our knowledge and understanding of the Holy One increases. Then, all our bitter water will become sweet.

Throughout our walk with God we must be ever on guard against selfishness. Our human love is fraught with it. Worming its way insidiously between the slightest chink in our armor, the self-life raises its ugly head to resist unqualified submission and dependence on the Lord. As we continue on our journey through the wilderness to Canaan, there will be ample opportunities to see the extent of our own selfishness.

The wilderness has the ability to burn through the smoothest and most polished veneer to reveal the innermost nature of man. God led His people through the wilderness for this very reason. Wanting His children stripped of every vain encumbrance so they would trust His love, God caused their weaknesses to come forth. Their sinful lack of faith lay bare beneath the desert sun.

It is essential for us to keep in mind that Jehovah God was not being callous. He saw the needs of the children of Israel and was providing for them. How much better it would be for them to realize the destructiveness of an uncrucified self-life by experiencing it. Self will struggle to the death to keep from admitting, "I cannot do it. I am too weak." Attempting to walk through life with our sense of worth based upon our accomplishments is worse than death.

To walk in faith, to be full of God, we must be empty of self. An unqualified, loving submission to the will of God in all circumstances requires an absolute crucifixion of every selfish tendency. The wilderness is a painful and oftentimes lonely experience, but it is an essential step in preparing us for the divine union. Every lesson learned enhances the richness of our fellowship with God.

After the people left the bitter waters of Marah they came to the oasis of Elim. God allowed them to camp there to regain their strength before venturing into the thorny plains of the Wilderness of Sin (pronounced *seen*). After a brief rest the people moved out. So vast was the multitude of people, and so sparse the sustenance provided by the desert, it was inevitable that the question of food would arise.

In response to their murmuring, for they did grumble and complain about their condition, God spoke the following words:

> Behold, I will rain bread from heaven for you. And the people shall go out and gather a certain quota every day, that I may test them, whether they will walk in My law or not.
>
> —EXODUS 16:4

Our heavenly Father did not condemn His people for murmuring. Instead, He explained the manner in which He would supply their needs.

God does not desire a once-and-for-all, everything-provided-for relationship with us. By responding to the call from Sinai, we have embarked on a lifelong journey, lived out one day at a time. Every step of the way is to be walked in the power of the Holy Spirit, in the footsteps of Jesus Christ. God's plan requires our *daily* dependence upon His unlimited resources. This bread from heaven, or *manna* as it was called, was the core of the Israelites' diet throughout their wilderness years.

The Lord Jesus spoke of bread many times to His disciples. He even performed miraculous feedings with loaves of bread. In His model prayer, Jesus said to pray in this way:

"Give us this day our daily bread" (Matthew 6:11). Another time when He was teaching, He told the disciples:

> "Most assuredly I say to you, Moses did not give you the bread from heaven, but My Father gives you the true bread from heaven. For the bread of God is He who comes down from heaven and gives life to the world"...Jesus said to them, "I am the bread of life. He who comes to Me shall never hunger, and he who believes in Me shall never thirst."
> —JOHN 6:32–33, 35

Daily communion with the living God is the privilege He desires to bestow on us. Like the Israelites, too often we do not believe God, and we try to "store up" time with Him instead of seeking it every day. We refuse to accept His utter faithfulness and the absolute truthfulness of His Word. God freely gives all that is necessary for the day.

While Israel was becoming accustomed to getting up early and gathering their daily bread before the sun could melt it, God led them out of the Wilderness of Sin. With this part of the journey behind them, the Israelites gladly made camp at Rephidim—until they realized there was no water.

There they were, bitter waters all over again, but this time without any water. When we read these few short chapters in Exodus, so filled with the miraculous power of God, it is inconceivable that the Israelites continued to complain. The children of Israel, only recently delivered from bondage, were beginning to learn of their Deliverer. As I look over my Christian growth I see the same pattern. My own attitude has shown a tendency to fluctuate between confident obedience to God's leading and a self-pitying, worrisome lack of faith. It requires time to grow in the knowledge of God and to develop a healthy, trusting relationship with Him.

At Rephidim, which means "refreshment," the people once again complained and murmured about their condition. Now that I recognized the similarities between my life and that of the Israelites, I could look through their shortcomings to God's timeless principles. So Moses cried, and God said,

> "Behold, I will stand before you there on the rock in Horeb; and you shall strike the rock, and water will come out of it, that the people may drink." And Moses did so in the sight of the elders of Israel.
>
> —EXODUS 17:6

As water flowed from the rock for the people to drink, they were refreshed. For every New Covenant believer, the symbolism of this miracle is of major importance. The rock is a type of Christ, as the Old Covenant prophet Isaiah fore-told of Jesus:

> Therefore thus says the LORD GOD: "Behold, I lay in Zion a stone for a foundation, a tried stone, a precious cornerstone, a sure foundation; Whoever believes will not act hastily."
>
> —ISAIAH 28:16

In Paul's first letter to the Corinthian church, he wrote:

> And all drank the same spiritual drink. For they drank of that spiritual Rock that followed them, and that Rock was Christ.
>
> —1 CORINTHIANS 10:4

Equally important as the rock was the manner in which the water was released. Moses was told to strike the rock. There is a beautiful passage in Isaiah foretelling how our Savior, the Lamb of God, would be struck down, which enhances our understanding of Moses' act. For the water of the Holy Spirit to flow freely, the Lamb had to be sacrificed.

It is from His wounds that the life-giving water comes to us.

> Surely He has borne our griefs and carried our sorrows; Yet we esteemed Him stricken, smitten by God, and afflicted. But He was wounded for our transgressions, He was bruised for our iniquities; the chastisement for our peace was upon Him, and by His stripes we are healed.
>
> —ISAIAH 53:4–5

The striking of the rock by Moses, and the wounding, beating, whipping and death of Jesus Christ, are essential elements of the call from Sinai. Without the water from the rock, the Israelites would have perished. Likewise, there would be no life-giving river flowing to a spiritually dead world through the body of believers had it not been for the sacrificial death of Jesus.

With our sins cleansed by the blood of the Lamb, we may dwell continuously at the Fountainhead of living waters. Our cups need never be anything less than overflowing. God desires that we enter into the crucified life of His Son. In that way we, through the anointing of the Holy Spirit, may convey His life to a lost world.

How often do we drink a glass of water without really tasting it? Without thinking about it, we tilt back the glass, and it's gone. At other times, especially after being out in the hot sun working up a good thirst, we savor every drop of that same glass of water. Cool, sparkling and refreshing, it tastes so good. We can imagine how good the water from the rock must have tasted to the weary Israelites.

Fresh from the thorny plains of Sin to Rephidim where the people suffered from the fearful lack of water, they cried out. God provided again, miraculously. We have seen how God often leads in these circuitous routes to prove His supernatural power and His unqualified, boundless love. Whenever He does, there waits in the shadow an enemy who would deceive the child of God.

Satan is a liar, a foul deceiver and a thief who, having failed to exalt himself above God, tries to steal and pervert every blessing God gives to His people. Even today, with his authority destroyed by the Lord of Glory, he harasses and attacks the weary saints. It was no different for the Israelites. While they made their camp at the place of refreshment, the enemy appeared.

The Scriptures tell us, "Now Amalek came and fought with Israel in Rephidim" (Exodus 17:8). First the blessing; then the attack. Before looking at the battle itself there are some important points we can learn from the name of this enemy tribe. According to the Hebrew lexicon, *Amel* means, "laborer, sufferer or workman."[1] From this we see that the Amalekites' tribal name meant "a people that grow weary from tireless labor and are destroyed by it." How often do we find ourselves in such circumstances, plodding along in our own strength, yet never gaining an inch—even losing ground? There is a rest that can, and must, be experienced by every Christian.

When those distant cousins attacked the children of Israel, Moses told Joshua:

> Choose us some men and go out, fight with Amalek. Tomorrow I will stand on the top of the hill with the rod of God in my hand.
> —EXODUS 17:9

Moses' hands, holding the rod, remained up, and the enemy was defeated. In this battle, there were two types of warfare taking place. It is appropriate that the enemies were called *Amalekites*, because one form of fighting was the wearisome toiling in human strength. The warriors exhibited the other form as they looked up to the finished work of Jesus (the rod of God held high). That is God's way. It is the march of faith.

So often when our enemies attack we find ourselves gauging their strength by the measure of human resources at our disposal. That is the surest, most effective way of entering the ranks of the defeated! Look at Moses. When he lowered his eyes to the carnage below, the enemy started winning. We are no different, especially living under the New Covenant.

"Come! Abide in Me." These two aspects of God's calling are revealed in this brief description. Under the Old Covenant, God's salvation was only a condition of their obedience, their works. If they obeyed God, He blessed them. If they didn't, He cursed them. How many people do we know who are perfect? Regardless of what the humanist movement, or the latest New Age psychologists would have us believe, perfection is less than a rarity. It is an impossibility, "for all have sinned and fall short of the glory of God" (Romans 3:23).

The defeat of the Israelites, a people working their way to victory, is the story of the Old Covenant. They fought the fight, but their confidence, their faith, was in the flesh. This way leads to failure or to the realization that we, in our own strength, cannot come to God, let alone abide continually in His presence. Paul the Apostle explains this in his letter to the Roman Christians. Speaking of the Law, the Old Covenant, he says:

> I was alive once without the law, but when the commandment came, sin revived and I died. And the commandment, which was to bring life, I found to bring death.
>
> —ROMANS 7:9–10

27

Like the children of Israel, we will find as we respond to God's calling, we cannot continue in our old ways—basking in the glory of our own accomplishments. The children of Israel learned this lesson by experience, and we most often learn by experience. By trying things our way—and failing—we begin to accept our need of a Savior. We pray, seek God's face, place our trust in Him and learn from Him. Our life of faith begins growing and flourishing. Certainly, battles must be fought, but they must be fought in the power of God.

When we do find ourselves being attacked by the enemy, it is usually important that we have the assistance of brothers and sisters in Christ to fight with us. Moses was not unaccompanied on Mount Tahuneh; Aaron and Hur were with him. Aaron symbolized the priestly order of the Old Testament and the priesthood of all believers, the Church of the New Testament. Hur, whose name means "white," represented the need for purity and righteousness in the lives of Old and New Covenant ministers.

We are told not to forsake the assembling together of the believers (Hebrews 10:25). It is the body of Christ that has the victory, and through its unity we are strengthened. In addition, we must learn to rest in the finished work of Christ. With the rod of God held high, Moses *sat down* upon the rock. Jesus is the Rock that is our sure foundation and precious Cornerstone upon whom we rest. We must, under the New Covenant, cease trying to earn the blessings of God. He alone is worthy, and He gives to us what we can never earn.

If I do not spend time with God, beginning early in the morning and continuing throughout the day, life seems harder, longer, drearier and less profitable. At the end of the day I am exhausted. On the other hand, when I seek God's presence early, admit my weaknesses to Him and rest in His strength, life is more enjoyable. No trouble seems insurmountable because I realize that God has already won the victory.

Triumphs such as the Israelites' victory over the Amalekites made great topics of discussion by weary travelers sitting around evening campfires. Who could resist telling the tale of this mighty God? He parted seas, brought water from solid rock and fought for His people. How this must have stirred the hearts of men as they listened in awe!

Eventually, one traveler's excited narrative reached the hungry ears of Jethro, Moses' father-in-law. In an instant, Jethro decided he would have to hear the entire story firsthand. Gathering together Moses' family, he set out to join the Israelites. Family reunions are typically joyous occasions, and this was no exception. After an emotional greeting and an exchange of pleasantries, they huddled in Moses' tent to hear the entire monumental story. Piece by incredible piece, the drama unfolded until, at its conclusion, Jethro, heart swelling with joy, proclaimed:

> Blessed be the LORD, who has delivered you out of the hand of the Egyptians and out of the hand of Pharaoh, and who has delivered the people from under the hand of the Egyptians. Now I know that the LORD is greater than all the gods; for in the very thing in which they behaved proudly, He was above them.
>
> —EXODUS 18:10–11

Whenever God's children come together to talk of His mighty exploits, of His faithfulness and love, hearts are lifted up. That is why fellowship is so important. God inhabits the praises of His people (Psalms 22:3). When men who are in love with Him turn their eyes heavenward, they, like Jethro, lift their voices in praise.

Pure spontaneous praise of this sort is so needed today in the body of Christ. Wounded, riddled with strife and division, we need to be healed. God is waiting to do just that. He calls, but we must respond. Look at Jethro. As he began to praise and worship God, Aaron came with the elders of Israel to share with them. The Lord drew His people—Moses, Aaron, Jethro and the elders—to worship Him together as one.

We read also of the early New Testament Church, so filled with mighty miracles and transformed lives. The believers were "with one accord in one place" (Acts 2:1). That is what God desires. The Scriptures further tell us:

> And they continued steadfastly in the apostles' doctrine and fellowship, in the breaking of bread, and in prayers…So continuing daily with one accord in the temple, and breaking bread from house to house, they ate their food with gladness and simplicity of heart, praising God and having favor with all the people. And the Lord added to the church daily those who were being saved.
>
> —ACTS 2:42, 46–47

God is the only One capable of taking a number of people and molding them, by His Spirit, into a healthy, growing, love-filled body. As a group of believers turn their gazes toward God and allow Him complete freedom to search every nook and cranny, every cobweb-laden closet of their hearts, God will reveal areas that need correcting. He did this for Moses and the Israelites through the astute observations of Jethro.

On his second day with Moses, Jethro watched as the Israelites resumed their usual routine. Beginning in the early morning hours, the people lined up to present their problems before God's spokesman. The Lord used Jethro to point out the weakness in such a practice.

> The thing that you do is not good. Both you and these people who are with you will surely wear yourselves out. For this thing is too much for you; you are not able to perform it by yourself.
>
> —EXODUS 18:17–18

The manner in which Moses received criticism is a credit to his humble, meek nature. "Now the man Moses was very humble, more than all men who were on the face of the earth" (Numbers 12:3). He did not respond out of pride, making reference to his chosen position as God's anointed leader. Instead, he listened, weighed the truth of Jethro's perception and implemented his father-in-law's suggestions. Here, though, is where he ran into difficulty. Just because the Lord used Jethro to reveal a need, it did not automatically mean the solution would come through him as well.

Jethro's recommendation did have some inherent strong points. He suggested to Moses:

> Listen now to my voice; I will give you counsel, and God will be with you: Stand before God for the people, so that you may bring the difficulties to God. And you shall teach them the statutes and the laws, and show them the way in which they must walk and the work they must do. Moreover you shall select from all the people able men, such as fear God, men of truth, hating covetousness; and place such over them to be rulers of thousands, rulers of hundreds, rulers of fifties, and rulers of tens.
>
> —EXODUS 18:19–21

This principle was essentially the one God later used to correct the situation, but it held one flaw. It had its roots in the wisdom of the world. Seemingly good advice is not always what it appears. We see only an infinitesimal piece of

God's plan, and neither His thoughts nor His ways are like ours. (See Isaiah 55:8–9.)

When God reveals something He wants to deal with, that is not a sign for us to barge ahead and do what we think must be done. It is, instead, a time to seek the Lord, to discern His will for the particular situation. Jethro, thinking as a man, based his suggestion upon good, sound, logical, rational common sense. True, he previously declared he knew Jehovah God was greater than all other gods. (See Exodus 18:11.) But Jethro still did not know *how* great God was.

Moses needed help, and Jethro's plan provided just that— nearly eighty thousand helpers! Without knowing God's heart, he could act no other way. The Lord is not pleased when His children place their trust in anything other than Him. Many years later, He warned through the prophet Isaiah,

> Woe to those who go down to Egypt for help, and rely on horses, who trust in chariots because they are many, and in horsemen because they are very strong, but who do not look to the Holy One of Israel, nor seek the LORD!
>
> —ISAIAH 31:1

Moses did not go to the Lord for answers. He only listened to his father-in-law's suggestion and then carried it out. God did allow it, and the plan may have helped for a time. It is hard to imagine, though, an organization with so many middlemen in management. The confusion must have been as staggering as it was time-consuming. Eventually, things reached the breaking point.

Approximately a year later, with Moses still bearing the bulk of the load, the Israelites grew weary of their steady diet of manna. When he heard their weeping, Moses sought the Lord, saying,

> Why have You afflicted Your servant? And why have
> I not found favor in Your sight, that You have laid the
> burden of all these people on me?...I am not able to
> bear all these people alone, because the burden is too
> heavy for me. If You treat me like this, please kill me
> here and now—if I have found favor in Your sight—
> and do not let me see my wretchedness!
> —NUMBERS 11:11, 14–15

God was waiting for those words. Then He could give Moses the plan *He* wished to institute. As long as Moses and the Israelites were content to struggle along with their own formulas, they missed out on God's best for them.

Our assessment of a situation may be accurate. So too the principles employed to correct the situation may be true. However, if we are not acting as God directs us and are not depending upon His resources, then we have missed out on the following precept: "'Not by might, nor by power, but by My Spirit,' says the LORD of hosts" (Zechariah 4:6). This is the key!

Never does God force His will upon any of His children. As it was with Moses, so it is with us. The moment Moses acknowledged his weakness and inability to continue, the Lord declared His perfect solution.

> Gather to Me seventy men of the elders of Israel,
> whom you know to be the elders of the people and
> officers over them; bring them to the tabernacle of
> meeting, that they may stand there with you. Then I
> will come down and talk with you there. I will take of
> the Spirit that is upon you and will put the same upon
> them; and they shall bear the burden of the people
> with you, that you may not bear it yourself alone.
> —NUMBERS 11:16–17

COME | *unto* | ME

Just seventy men with the anointing of God upon them could replace Jethro's eighty thousand! How like the children of Israel we are. Too often we learn the hard way, taking things into our own hands, presuming upon God's grace and expecting Him to bless our efforts.

I am beginning to learn that whenever I must make organizational decisions, I should try to follow the principle of asking the Lord for His ideas first. God alone knows all the details, and He alone has all the answers. If I am to make the correct choice, I must seek the Lord's will with an open heart and mind, ready to follow His guidance, regardless of the cost. Any success that St. Luke's has enjoyed is because it was born of, and is directed by God. My goal always is to let the Holy Spirit be our *Office Manager*, while I and the other employees are servants. This is the secret of success.

We can rest assured that the Lord is dedicated to helping each of us succeed in our calling. He committed Himself to bring His children out of Egypt to the mountain, and then on to the land of milk and honey. He has made the same commitment to us today. Who could imagine the tremendous cost of such commitment? We have this much of an advantage over the Israelites—we know the cost. God became flesh and blood to die in our place. With open arms and a heart of love, He still calls us out of bondage to Himself, to experience continually the fullness of His love. As our knowledge of Him grows, we will begin to trust in Him with our whole heart. He, in turn, as we acknowledge Him, will direct our every step. (See Proverbs 3:5–6.)

CHAPTER 4

Meeting with the Master

God sent Moses to Pharaoh, fully intending to bring the Israelites back to Himself. He promised Moses, "When you have brought the people out of Egypt, you shall serve God on this mountain" (Exodus 3:12). Mount Sinai was only a stopping place on their way to the Promised Land, but it was by far the most important stop.

The first leg of the journey lay behind them. God had taught them some basic principles by which they were to live, and He showed them that He was greater than every circumstance they would encounter.

Now they were to learn that God wanted fellowship. While the Israelites camped at the foot of Mount Sinai, Moses received the following reminder from the Lord:

> You have seen what I did to the Egyptians, and how I bore you on eagles' wings, and brought you to Myself. Now therefore, if you will indeed obey My voice and keep My covenant, then you shall be a special treasure to Me above all people; for all the earth is Mine. And you shall be to Me a kingdom of priests and a holy nation.
>
> —EXODUS 19:4–6

There were those words, "*I brought you to Myself.*" God led the Israelites out, wanting them to enter that special place He had set aside for them. The offer was made, the promise extended and the conditions stated. Obedience!

The people heard these words and readily agreed. Without considering the cost, and without the slightest hesitation, they declared, "All that the LORD has spoken we will do!" (Exodus 19:8). Certainly their intentions were good, and the thought of being a *kingdom of priests and a holy nation* was sufficient enticement to warrant their desire for obedience. Their hearts were in the right place, but they did not yet understand the total transformation His holy love demanded.

God told Moses to get the people prepared for their meeting. To come into His presence they had to sanctify themselves and put aside all uncleanness for three days. Then God would descend upon the mountain and speak to Moses in their sight. Were they as ready for this encounter as they believed themselves to be? From the account in Scripture, it is obvious they were not.

> Then it came to pass on the third day, in the morning, that there were thunderings and lightnings, and a thick cloud on the mountain; and the sound of the trumpet was very loud, so that all the people who were in the camp trembled. And Moses brought the people out of the camp to meet with God, and they stood at the foot of the mountain. Now Mount Sinai was completely in smoke, because the LORD descended upon it in fire. Its smoke ascended like the smoke of a furnace, and the whole mountain quaked greatly.
>
> —EXODUS 19:16–18

Even from where they stood at the foot of Mount Sinai,

the reality of God's presence was overpowering. Thunder rocked the mountain to its foundation as fingers of lightning played upon the peaks. This was too much for the Israelites to take, especially without the comforting presence of either Moses or Aaron.

What happened while these two men of God were in the heights above? Even as God was declaring to them the Ten Commandments, the hearts of the Israelites were growing faint and their knees weak.

> Now all the people witnessed the thunderings, the lightning flashes, the sound of the trumpet, and the mountain smoking; and when the people saw it, they trembled and stood afar off.
>
> —EXODUS 20:18

God brought them to the mountain to meet with Him, but they chose not to remain. Nothing in the land of Egypt or their wilderness experience had prepared them for this. When Moses returned to them from the mountain, they were quick to say: "You speak with us, and we will hear; but let not God speak with us, lest we die" (Exodus 20:19).

There is a message here that every born-again Christian should understand. Although it is easier to be taught *about* God by another person, that is only *second best*. That is the way of the Old Covenant, where the priests were the only ones allowed into the tabernacle. It is not the way of the New. God calls each of His children into His presence to hear the voice of His Holy Spirit, to learn of Him and to experience His love. Yes, we are to submit to the Church's divinely appointed leadership, but we are all to experience the fullness of a personal relationship with Him. In fact, because of Jesus, we can now come boldly before the throne of grace (Hebrews 4:16).

How it must have grieved the Father-heart of God when His children ran in fear. How much more it must grieve Him today when we refuse to come to Him.

The presence of God is such that no man can enter it without being transformed. The Israelites sensed this. They knew that if they remained near the mountain their inner-most selves would be exposed. Then, if they remained, their selfish desires would fall aside, hindrances would dissolve and they would become new creatures. When this realization dawned on them, any thought of their earlier promises of obedience faded.

With the establishing of the Law and the Ten Commandments came a new way of life. It was not intended to bring them into bondage. On the contrary, it was meant to set them free from every selfish delusion, to open their eyes to the awesome holiness of God and to make prepara-tion for the coming Messiah. By pointing out God's call to holiness and man's inability to be holy in his own strength, the stage was set for the need of a Savior. Even as Christians, we experience the results of that same call.

At the moment of our second birth we begin trying to serve God. We know very little about Him, but we give Him everything we have—including ourselves—and He leads us to the mountain to meet with Him. We, like the Israelites, must come to God and allow Him free rein in our hearts. We have an advantage over the Israelites of old because Jesus Christ sent the Holy Spirit to live and work within us. He gives the strength to endure the death of self and the uniting into the wounds of the Crucified One. As we saw earlier, death must come before new life can freely flow.

Jesus Christ, the Messiah, came to fulfill the require-ments of the Old Covenant Law. In His Sermon on the Mount, He told the assembled multitudes:

Do not think that I came to destroy the Law or the Prophets. I did not come to destroy but to fulfill. For assuredly I say to you, till heaven and earth pass away, one jot or one tittle will by no means pass from the law till all is fulfilled.

—MATTHEW 5:17–18

IMPORTANT PRINCIPLES FROM MOUNT SINAI

Mount Sinai holds such significance for the child of God that it is hard to say which particular aspect is central to all else. They are all important. There are, however, several points that form a distinctive core of truth we should whole-heartedly embrace. Some of these we have already touched upon, so now we can bring them into focus to see what the overall picture reveals.

The giving of the Law and its fulfillment by Jesus Christ began on Mount Sinai in an encounter with the Living God. We mentioned how the Old Covenant was to prepare the way for the New by revealing to each of us our own sinful nature. Even living under the New Covenant of grace, this mountaintop experience must take place within every believer. Just because we have been saved by grace does not automatically open the doors to heavenly blessings. We can still be living in bondage to the Old Covenant method of salvation by works alone.

Even worse than this is the possibility of giving in to the all-too-common philosophy that holiness is beyond our grasp. Or, as the devil would have us believe, that because we are forgiven we need not worry about those little beset-ting sins. The devil would try to convince us that it is beyond our capacity to live holy lives. It is true that by an act of grace, the blood of Jesus cleanses us from our sin. However, when Jesus fulfilled the Law, He simply made it possible, through the power of the Holy Spirit, for every believer to be holy. If we "walk in the Spirit," we will not "fulfill the lust of the flesh" (Galatians 5:16).

Jehovah is greater than anything the Israelites, or we, could comprehend. God told Moses that if they obeyed Him they would be a particular people, holding a special place in His kingdom. Under the New Covenant we are also given a special place in the kingdom of God—as heirs! But to have all the power of God working within us we need first to accept the Old Covenant teaching—death to the self-life. Then we must let the Holy Spirit lead us from death, through the wounds in the Vine (Jesus), to His life.

Let us not think even for a moment that this is an easy experience. The children of Israel trembled in fear and withdrew. Even so, God did not desert them. He gave them the Law, the commandments, directions for building an altar and the pattern for worship in the wilderness tabernacle. When they left Mount Sinai carrying the Ark of the Covenant, they went knowing that without a doubt God was among them. Are we any different? Certainly not. All who respond to the call from Sinai, who come to the mountain in faithful obedience, will leave with the blessed assurance that God is with them.

We are reminded once more that we can come to meet God on the mountain only because Jesus has fulfilled the Law's requirements. As Christians we do not have to make a pilgrimage to the geological location of Sinai, but we have a meeting with Him in our heart. The writer of the letter of the Hebrews wrote to the New Covenant believers of his day—and to every Christian forever—these words:

> For you have not come to the mountain that may
> be touched and that burned with fire, and to black-
> ness and darkness and tempest, and the sound of a

trumpet and the voice of words, so that those who heard it begged that the word should not be spoken to them anymore…But you have come to Mount Zion and to the city of the living God, the heavenly Jerusalem, to an innumerable company of angels, to the general assembly and church of the firstborn who are registered in heaven, to God the Judge of all, to the spirits of just men made perfect, to Jesus the Mediator of the new covenant, and to the blood of sprinkling that speaks better things than that of Abel. See that you do not refuse Him who speaks. For if they did not escape who refused Him who spoke on earth, much more shall we not escape if we turn away from Him who speaks from heaven, whose voice then shook the earth; but now He has promised, saying, "Yet once more I shake not only the earth, but also heaven."

—HEBREWS 12:18–19, 22–26

This passage will have its literal fulfillment when God establishes His everlasting kingdom, but He does not expect us to wait until then before coming to learn of Him and abide in Him. He desires this for us now.

There are other lessons to be learned from the meeting on the mountain. While God was giving Moses such revelation, something managed to sneak into the camp below. Today, we know this enemy by the name of "humanism." Its ways are subtle. Often we do not recognize the treachery of this thief until it is too late.

Humanism plays upon and feeds the selfish prideful desires of human nature. Anytime we choose to follow the ways of man, the wisdom of the world or the desires of the flesh as opposed to the sovereign will of God, we are guilty. At other times, by attempting to serve God while relying on our own strength, we fall prey. No one is exempt from this temptation, especially in these days, and we can afford to leave no door open to wayward thoughts. The answer lies in the cross of our Lord.

Jesus Christ died, but He is no longer in the tomb. It is empty! When we become united to the Vine, when we are one with His death, we are also one with His life. The children of Israel could not face this. While Moses was on the mountain with God they gave in to fear, and their trust in God failed. They took things into their own hands and surrendered to humanistic tendencies. Scripture tells us,

> Now when the people saw that Moses delayed coming down from the mountain, the people gathered together to Aaron, and said to him, "Come, make us gods that shall go before us; for as for this Moses, the man who brought us up out of the land of Egypt, we do not know what has become of him."
> —EXODUS 32:1

Called to faithfully await the return of their leader, they failed. With their eyes on Moses instead of God, the Israelites gave in to the lies of Satan. If their gaze had been focused upon God, there would have been no room for fear. As it was, with the onslaught of fear came the temptation to work things out themselves. Having chosen to remain at a safe distance from God's presence, they limited their experience of His loving Father-heart. The door was open, not to victory and blessing, but to humanism and defeat.

They made their own god—a calf of gold—and brought upon themselves the wrath of God. It seemed easier to have a god they could see and touch, one who would not shake them to their very roots. In the end, what a price they paid! The Lord was so angry He wanted to destroy the entire nation of Israel and to begin again with Moses. (See Exodus 32:10.) If not for the intercession of that faithful man of God, it surely would have occurred. Instead, those who succumbed to idolatry and would not repent were slain by the swords of the faithful.

When many people look at such a passage of Scripture, they focus only upon the wrath of God. There is a danger in this. He is much more than a God of vengeance. His method of dealing with sin under the Law was sudden and sure; it simply could not be tolerated. There was a vital lesson being taught in a deadly war with Satan. How often we overlook the anguish our shortsightedness must have upon God when all we can see is His judgment!

The Israelites suffered from this problem. They could not see through God's judgment to His heart of love. We who have experienced God's saving grace have the opposite problem to overcome. Our task is to see through His love to impending judgment upon sin. There is a balance that the Christian needs. The same God who destroyed three thousand Israelites because of their sin is the same One who sent His Son to die for all sin.

When Aaron, the high priest, created the golden calf, it symbolized the infiltration of humanism into the body of Christ. No longer just a philosophy, the religion of humanism is destroying much of the modern church. Many leaders no longer preach the deadly results of sin. Instead, they "tickle the ears" of the membership with only pleasant, comforting messages. There is no place for humanism in the Christian life. We are called to holiness. The Word of God tells us,

> But as He who called you is holy, you also be holy in all your conduct, because it is written, *"Be holy, for I am holy."*
>
> —1 PETER 1:15–16, EMPHASIS ADDED

As we encounter the presence of almighty God, every fiber of our being will come under His probing gaze. Jehovah God wants to open our lives and fill us with His very own life, but He leaves that decision up to us. Never will He force His presence, His love or His power upon us! The choice is in our hands. Will we allow our selfish human nature to drive us in fear from the Lord, or will we submit to Him? Trusting in God's love, dare we also accept His baptism of fire? He calls us from the heights of Mount Sinai, but it is not mere thunder and lightning He wishes to place within our hearts. The gift is nothing less than Himself, for it is written, "Our God is a consuming fire" (Hebrews 12:29). What will your choice be?

CHAPTER 5

Hard Lessons

I n preparation for the conquest of Canaan, God called Moses back to the top of Mt. Sinai. Jehovah God's commitment to His people went beyond their rebellion and lack of faith. It went beyond eternity. He promised, and it would be fulfilled. The land of Canaan was destined for Israel from the moment God told Abraham it would be theirs (Genesis 12:5–7). Now that the time was near, God revealed some of the details as to how He would accomplish this. Scripture tells us that God responded to Moses' intercession by saying:

> Behold, I am going to make a covenant. Before all your people I will perform miracles which have not been produced in all the earth, nor among any of the nations; and all the people among whom you live will see the working of the LORD, for it is a fearful thing that I am going to perform with you. Be sure to observe what I am commanding you this day: behold, I am going to drive out the Amorite before you, and the Canaanite, the Hittite, the Perizzite, the Hivite and the Jebusite. Watch yourself that you make no covenant with the inhabitants of the land into which you are going, lest it become a snare in your midst.

> But rather, you are to tear down their altars and
> smash their sacred pillars and cut down their
> Asherim—for you shall not worship any other god,
> for the LORD, whose name is Jealous, is a jealous God.
> —EXODUS 34:10–14, NAS

This was the bottom line. God was going to work miraculously. All He required in return was their loving obedience.

How faithfully did they follow? When God gave the command to march forward, the children of Israel eagerly set out for the Promised Land. Little did they realize it would be another thirty-eight years before the conquest of Canaan would begin. Full of trust and confidence there at the mountain, it was easy to believe God for miracles.

However, rebellion by way of pride is one of the most troublesome areas for every child of God. Even in the most anointed of ministries, precautions must be taken to guard against the tactics of Satan. Whenever there is an open door, wherever any of our fleshly nature remains uncrucified, he will entice. Satan would have us believe we do not need to submit to one another in love (Ephesians 5:21), or that we are equally or better qualified than those in authority over us. No one is exempt from such temptation. Until the day Satan is cast into the lake of fire, he will do what he can to steal, kill and destroy.

Aaron, Moses' high priest, again allowed himself to be swayed by the devil's leading. He and Miriam—Moses' own brother and sister—rebelled against Moses' authority as God's chosen leader.

> Then Miriam and Aaron spoke against Moses
> because of the Ethiopian woman whom he had married; for he had married an Ethiopian woman. So
> they said, "Has the LORD indeed spoken only

through Moses? Has He not spoken through us also?"
And the LORD heard it.

—NUMBERS 12:1–2

Satan will use anything and anyone he can to cause the
saints to stumble and fall. In this case it was prejudice against
Moses' wife. Once they allowed a single question to enter
their thoughts, another soon followed, all the way to out-
right rebellion. We need to take another look at the last few
words of verse twelve, "And the Lord heard it." We can
make no mistake about this. Our sin will not remain hidden
forever. God knew their thoughts. He heard their words, and
He dealt with the problem.

Moses, unaware perhaps of his family's feelings, was
called, along with Miriam and Aaron, to appear before God.
The Scripture tells us that God not only spoke, but that He
spoke *suddenly* (Numbers 12:4). For all time, any doubt was
settled regarding Moses' unique position before God.

> Then He said, "Hear now My words:
>
> If there is a prophet among you,
> I, the LORD, make Myself known to him in a vision;
> I speak to him in a dream.
> Not so with My servant Moses;
> He is faithful in all My house.
> I speak with him face to face,
> Even plainly, and not in dark sayings;
> And he sees the form of the LORD.
> Why then were you not afraid
> To speak against My servant Moses?"

—NUMBERS 12:6–8

Because of Miriam's critical attitude, she became
instantly leprous. Once again, only through the prayerful
intercession of Moses, was God's anger appeased. Had Moses

not cried out on her behalf, she would have continued as a leper and been cast away from the camp. This is how serious rebellion is in God's eyes.

Every step of the way, Jehovah God was teaching the children of Israel principles that would insure their success in the Promised Land. However, not all of the people were willing to receive His teachings. They failed to grasp the one essential of pleasing God: Their faith did not grow beyond that which their eyes could see. Nowhere was this more evident than while the Israelites camped in the wilderness of Paran, discussing the spies' report.

It was there in the wilderness of Paran that God commanded Moses to send twelve men, one of the heads of each tribe, into Canaan to spy out the land. For forty days they searched through the land of milk and honey, determining its strength and weaknesses, to see what it would take to conquer it. When the spies returned they brought back some of the luscious fruits found in Canaan, and they declared, "We went to the land where you sent us...and this is its fruit" (Numbers 13:27). They also brought back something else—a divided report.

Into the hands of every child of God is given a truly awesome power. "Death and life are in the power of the tongue, and those who love it will eat its fruit" (Proverbs 18:21). With one choice, we can nullify every miracle He would perform. God loves us that much. He will not force even so much as a victory upon us. We must recognize that with this power comes responsibility. No longer may we claim ignorance of the subject—should we choose to doubt we will surely suffer. It was so with the Israelites, and it is the same today. As it is written, "The just shall live by faith" (Galatians 3:11; cf: Hebrews 10:38).

The spies returned from Canaan, and ten of the twelve were overwhelmed with unbelief. God had already promised

to fight for them and drive out their enemies before them
(Exodus 34:11), but they lost sight of Him. All they saw were
giants, walled cities and their own weakness in comparison.
Amidst all this unbelief, God still retained a seed of faith.
Caleb exhorted the people, "Let us go up at once and take
possession, for we are well able to overcome it" (Numbers
13:30). His appeal was swallowed up by their fear.

When the Israelites faced the choice of believing God to
fulfill His promises or believing what the ten spies had seen,
they succumbed to the evil report given by the ten. Despite
past miracles, one after another, the children of Israel lacked
true faith. They did not know God's heart of love would
never let them down. He could never forsake His own. This
truth failed to become rooted in them. From the moment
they accepted the words of the ten spies, they were doomed.

> We are not able to go up against the people, for they
> are stronger than we...There we saw the giants (the
> descendants of Anak came from the giants); and we
> were like grasshoppers in our own sight, and so we
> were in their sight.
>
> —Numbers 13:31, 33

The Israelites saw themselves as insignificant and power-
less instead of who they were in truth—children of *El Elyon*,
the Most High God. Unbelief destroyed them. An entire
generation perished before ever entering the Promised Land
because they would not have faith in God. They could have
believed. They had that choice in front of them, and the
ensuing responsibility. Unbelief, rebellion and ultimately
death were theirs at their own choosing. Only faithful Joshua
and Caleb would enter the land of milk and honey. They
were the only two who took God at His Word, and He
rewarded their unquestioning faith.

How far removed are we from those chosen ones? Every Christian should be able to look back at the record of God's faithfulness and have no trouble believing His promises. Too often, though, this is not the case. The Lord promises that we should walk triumphantly through every situation because we are in Christ (2 Corinthians 2:14). He gives us the victory through Himself because at Calvary He destroyed Satan's authority (1 Corinthians 15:57). There is no reason for us to waste away wandering endlessly in the wilderness, but the possibility looms in our path, should we choose to doubt.

We are God's children. Through the blood of the Lamb, we are as much His as the Israelites. Their rebellion could not be tolerated, and neither can ours. I have learned that in every aspect of my life, to the degree that I identify with God and His boundless abilities, I succeed. The moment I begin questioning my oneness with Him, the door to unbelief opens, and I fail. No longer am I walking by faith, and life ceases to glow with fulfillment. The victory is lost.

This does not mean that we will not experience difficulties. On the contrary, Jesus told His followers to expect tribulation. As long as we are in this world we cannot escape trials and tribulations. Jesus said so, but He also said, right after that: "Take courage; I have overcome the world" (John 16:33, NAS). Like the Israelites, every time the enemy attacks, each time God allows us to be tested, ultimately we are supposed to be victorious. In Christ, hid in His shadow and secure in His loving embrace, there can be nothing but victory. If we will abide in Him and not rebel when the fire in the furnace of affliction is fanned, He will always cause us to triumph.

Continuing their wilderness wanderings, the children of Israel came to the desert of Sin. Here it was that another dry spell came upon them. They faced a lack of water and little, if any, food, so they gave in to that same devastating sin of unbelief. Even under a divinely imposed death sentence, the Israelites failed to repent and trust God wholeheartedly. Instead, they chose to complain again to Moses and Aaron.

Moses and Aaron fell on their faces before the Lord, imploring His mercy and His miracles. God replied:

> Take the rod; you and your brother Aaron gather the congregation together. Speak to the rock before their eyes, and it will yield its water; thus you shall bring water for them out of the rock, and give drink to the congregation and their animals.
>
> —NUMBERS 20:8

We should be careful to notice that they were not to strike the rock as they did at Rephidim. They were only to speak and believe. Up until that time Moses had flawlessly obeyed the Lord. If not for him, the nation of Israel would have been destroyed several times over. He learned his lessons well, but he was still a man with human frailties. He was subject to mistakes. The One who is perfect had not yet come.

Gathering the people together as God commanded, Moses took the rod and said, "Hear now, you rebels! Must we bring water for you out of this rock?" (Numbers 20:10). Notice his words, "Must we bring…" Moses had started thinking it was his own efforts that had brought success before, and they would work again. Somehow, whether through anger, frustration, impatience or pride, a way was opened for Satan's influence. Perhaps, since water out of the rock was not an entirely new experience for Moses, his confidence was in the method already tried and proven instead of in the Lord. The responsibility for what occurred fell squarely on Moses' shoulders.

When God directed Moses and Aaron to do something new (speak to the rock instead of strike it), that is exactly what He meant. As leader of the people, it was Moses' duty to see that the Lord's commands were obeyed. Instead, he disobeyed.

> Then Moses lifted his hand and struck the rock twice with his rod; and water came out abundantly, and the congregation and their animals drank.
>
> —NUMBERS 20:11

To fully understand the implications of this passage, we must reconsider the spiritual significance of the first time God released water from the rock at Rephidim. On that occasion, He did instruct Moses to strike the rock. We saw how the rock symbolized the coming Messiah—the rock was struck, as Jesus would be (Isaiah 53:4, 8). When Moses hit the rock at Rephidim, life-giving water gushed forth to save the Israelites from dying of thirst. How prophetic this was of Jesus' words to the woman at the well centuries later:

> Whoever drinks of this water will thirst again, but whoever drinks of the water that I shall give him will never thirst. But the water that I shall give him will become in him a fountain of water springing up into everlasting life.
>
> —JOHN 4:13–14

Right after Jesus cried from the cross of Calvary, "It is finished!" a soldier pierced His side with a spear and "immediately blood and water came out" (John 19:30, 34). Following His Resurrection and Ascension to heaven, Jesus sent the life-giving water of the Holy Spirit to those who believed in Him.

Now we can begin to dig for hidden pearls. If the first

incident at Rephidim, where Moses struck the rock, symbolized the crucifixion of Jesus and the spiritual life that flows from Him, what about the meaning of the second time? Why was God so angry with Moses for doing the same act as before? Even though God responded and brought forth water out of the rock for the people to drink, Moses was not allowed to lead the people into the Promised Land because of his disobedience. (See Numbers 12:20.) (Num 20:12)

How many times can a man be crucified? Jesus was a man, yet He was God incarnate. He was crucified *only once* to pay for the sins of humanity *forever*. Never again would daily animal sacrifices be required as in the Old Testament. The shedding of blood from His perfect life was enough to blot out the sins of all people everywhere. To crucify Jesus physically again (to strike the rock twice) would not only be impossible, but unnecessary and humiliating to Him.

> For in the case of those who have once been enlightened and have tasted of the heavenly gift and have been made partakers of the Holy Spirit, and have tasted of the good word of God and the powers of the age to come, and then have fallen away, it is impossible to renew them again to repentance, since they again crucify to themselves the Son of God and put Him to open shame.
> —HEBREWS 6:4–6, NAS

Jesus Christ made provision for all at Calvary. He was crucified, and He sent the Holy Spirit as rivers of living water to flow out of believers. From that moment forth we must receive, by faith, the promises of God and remove, by faith, the obstacles—by declaring them with our mouths. We speak to our Rock, Jesus Christ, and declare the life-giving truth of His Word in every situation. (This is not related to the unbalanced teaching of simply "confessing and claim-ing" material luxuries.)

> Whoever says to this mountain, "Be removed and be
> cast into the sea," and does not doubt in his heart,
> but believes that those things he says will be done,
> he will have whatever he says.
>
> —MARK 11:23

When water was needed again to quench the Israelites' thirst, the Father wanted to release it on the basis of an accomplished fact. Once the Rock, Jesus, had likewise already been stricken, the reservoir of God's unfathomable riches lay waiting to be unleashed. The key is called *faith*. Into the hands of God's people this key is given. Dare we accept what Jesus Christ accomplished nearly two thousand years ago? The alternative is to take part in Moses' failure. He was denied the privilege of leading God's people into the land of milk and honey. What a terrible price we will pay if we should deny the effectiveness of the cross of Christ.

This is a common point of attack for the humanistic and New Age movements, inspired by the spirit of the antichrist. The cross is where the victory was accomplished, and Satan tries to use these philosophies to destroy its power by diluting our faith in it. Surely it was not by natural sight that Moses was to see this truth. When he looked at the rock, that was all he saw—a rock. However, God called him to see beyond their present circumstances to the unseen, eternal things. We are called, every one of us, to this same walk of faith.

Every time we choose to believe God alone, we allow the Holy Spirit freedom to begin to develop godly character within us. At one point in my career, the Lord led me through a couple of faith and character-building exercises. Several other doctors and hospitals ran some misleading advertisements, inflating the patient's bill to Medicare and then discounting it to appear "cost-free" for the patient. Even after the "reduction," the cost to Medicare was still $1000 more than what St. Luke's charged for the identical procedure. As you can imagine, this created some tough competition and touchy situations. God was faithful, though. We survived by adhering to basic Christian principles and the direction of our "Office Manager," the Holy Spirit.

Another personal test of faith happened one Christmas a few years ago. During an especially severe winter, nearly three thousand acres of citrus in which I had invested were destroyed by frost. There were no obvious reasons why. I cried out to God. In time, He not only provided an answer, but a lesson. My faith in Him was to be independent of worldly possessions, and besides, He had other plans for that land. I have learned that His ways are perfect. Only through intimacy with Him have my eyes been able to see the "unseen."

While the Jews journeyed from Mount Hor around the land of Edom they suffered another bout of grumbling. As a direct consequence of their sin, "The LORD sent fiery serpents among the people, and they bit the people; and many of the people of Israel died" (Numbers 21:6). Their complaining and rebellion allowed Satan to wreak havoc among them. When they acknowledged their sin and repented of it, God made a way of escape. They were to make a bronze serpent and place it upon a pole. Anyone who was bitten had only to look up at the bronze replica, and he would be healed.

It is important to notice that when the Israelites repented of their sin, God did not remove the troublesome serpents from their midst. He could have, but He chose to leave them.

They would serve as instruments to test and perfect the people. This was perhaps similar to the apostle Paul's thorn in the flesh, which remained in spite of his prayers so that he would be kept from exalting himself. (See 2 Corinthians 12:7.) By faithfully doing what God told them to do, the Israelites could be healed. If they refused to look up at the bronze serpent, they died.

At first glance, we may think it strange that God would require His children to look at a graven image of a serpent in order to be healed. Satan, disguised as a serpent, had tempted Eve in the Garden of Eden and thereby caused the fall of the entire human race. Does this mean that sometimes God will use idols to heal us? Certainly not. Once again, God's instructions symbolically foreshadowed His Son.

On the cross, Jesus actually became, or took on, the sins of mankind (represented by the serpent). "He made Him who knew no sin to be sin for us, that we might become the righteousness of God in Him" (2 Corinthians 5:21). Jesus suffered beyond comprehension for our salvation. No work is necessary on our part to receive His gift of healing, physically and spiritually—we merely need to look up to Jesus Christ.

CHAPTER 6

Onward to Victory

D uring the years in the wilderness, the unfaithful children of Israel perished, and Jehovah God raised up a brand-new generation. They had never learned the pleasures of Egypt and were able to identify more closely with the Lord, beginning to see things from His perspective. Gone were most of the seeds of doubt and the roots of rebellion. This time when the call came to cross the Jordan and go in to possess the land of milk and honey, the majority of them wholeheartedly agreed with those two devoted servants, Joshua and Caleb.

Neither walled cities nor giants could deter them. Joshua and Caleb were realistic enough to see the well-protected fortresses, the giants and the many races of strong people who would oppose them. However, they remained undaunted. The courageous pair counted on the Lord to win the victory. *That* is faith!

We recall that the greater number of Israelites who left Mt. Sinai with Moses to embark on the wilderness journey were only partially committed to God, but they still expected Him to establish their works. Such was the case with the tribes of Reuben, Gad and one-half of the tribe of Manasseh. They too had heard of the wonderful land of

Canaan and of the tremendous fruit that Joshua and Caleb brought back from their scouting trip. Yet the descendants of these two and one-half tribes preferred to remain on the east side of the Jordan River rather than cross over into the Promised Land.

These sheep and goat farmers were attracted to the fertile grazing lands located east of the Jordan. Instead of trusting God to make provision for them in Canaan, they elected to go with the visible, tangible good. ("A bird in the hand is worth two in the bush" could have been their motto.) They decided to go to Moses and make their requests known. He had lived through the disastrous effects of their ancestor's rebellion and was quick to point out the resemblance to them.

> But Moses said to the sons of Gad and to the sons of Reuben, "Shall your brothers go to war while you yourselves sit here? Now why are you discouraging the sons of Israel from crossing over into the land which the LORD has given them?...Now behold, you have risen up in your fathers' place, a brood of sinful men, to add still more to the burning anger of the LORD against Israel. For if you turn away from following Him, He will once more abandon them in the wilderness; and you will destroy all these people."
>
> —NUMBERS 32:6–7, 14–15, NAS

Their request was, in reality, a subtle form of rebellion. They were unwilling to unite with the rest of Israel in following the Lord's direction. In response to the rebuke of Moses, they offered a compromise. The tribes of Reuben, Gad and the half-tribe of Manasseh agreed to go forward into Canaan and fight with the rest if they would be allowed to return and settle with their families across the river (Numbers 32:17-18). Moses accepted their offer and instructed his successor, Joshua, to make sure they honored their agreement.

In order for us to appreciate the magnitude of God's command to cross the Jordan River, it may be helpful to understand a little geography of the area. The Jordan is a very long river—probably one hundred fifty to two hundred miles long, and it has its beginning in the cavern of Phiala in northern Palestine at the foot of Mount Lebanon. From there it runs underground to Caesarea Philippi, where the Lord Jesus said, "and on this rock" (of revelation that He was the Christ) "I will build My church, and the gates of Hades shall not prevail against it" (Matthew 16:18). At Caesarea Philippi the Jordan breaks out and flows approximately fifteen miles south to Lake Marom and into the Sea of Galilee. Finally, it reaches the Dead Sea. In some places the river is sixty to one hundred feet wide and six to ten feet deep. During the spring it overflows its banks and is most difficult to cross. Of course it was precisely at this time of year that God commanded the Israelites to cross the Jordan and enter the Promised Land.

The Lord demanded active participation, courage and obedience from Joshua and the people. As at the Red Sea, He performed the miracle. This time He waited until those carrying the Ark of the Covenant stepped from dry land into the raging currents. In contrast to the Red Sea crossing, the people were to follow far enough behind the ark so that every member of the vast multitude could see it. This ark, carried by the priests and Levites, was their guide. When it moved, they moved. We read in the book of Joshua:

> And they commanded the people, saying, "When you see the ark of the covenant of the LORD your God, and the priests, the Levites, bearing it, then you shall set out from your place and go after it. Yet there shall be a space between you and it, about two thousand cubits by measure. Do not come near it,

> that you may know the way by which you must go,
> for you have not passed this way before."
>
> —JOSHUA 3:3-4

After Joshua told the people where to look for guidance on their journey, he gave them another command:

> Sanctify yourselves, for tomorrow the LORD will do wonders among you.
>
> —JOSHUA 3:5

Joshua knew that God is a holy God as well as a God of miracles. He would not tolerate any unclean thing in His presence, especially among His people. Having already received the ceremonial laws, the Israelites were to undergo a cleansing ritual the day before the crossing in preparation for the miracle.

Early the next morning, with everything in readiness, the people watched and waited eagerly for the sign. How many straining eyes must have searched the horizon that day! They had already been told that the waters would dry up as soon as the priests stepped into the river. So they waited, wondering, *How much longer would it be?* Suddenly, excitement nearing the breaking point, things began to happen. The ark was moving toward the river!

> So it came about when the people set out from their tents to cross the Jordan with the priests carrying the ark of the covenant before the people, and when those who carried the ark came into the Jordan, and the feet of the priests carrying the ark were dipped in the edge of the water (for the Jordan overflows its banks all the days of harvest), that the waters which were flowing down from above stood and rose up in one heap, a great distance away at Adam, the city that is beside Zarethan; and those

which were flowing down toward the sea of the
Arabah, the Salt Sea, were completely cut off. So
the people crossed opposite Jericho. And the priests
who carried the ark of the covenant of the LORD
stood firm on dry ground in the middle of the
Jordan while all Israel crossed on dry ground, until
all the nation had finished crossing the Jordan.

—JOSHUA 3:14–17, NAS

Hallelujah! God performed His promised miracle. He
stilled the raging currents and transformed them into firm,
dry ground so His people could pass over to Canaan. After
forty long years in the Sinai wilderness, the land of milk and
honey was theirs to conquer.

Sitting there atop Mount Sinai, I could not see the
Jordan River, but I could ponder its significance. This river
not only separated the wilderness from the Promised Land,
but it marked another distinctive change in the Israelites.
Prior to the crossing of the Jordan there was conflict resulting in defeat. After the crossing, there was conflict resulting
in victory. The forty years in the wilderness had effected
change in their relationship with God. They were now ready
to submit to the will of the Lord and respond eagerly to His
calling.

Peering into the distance toward that unseen river, I con-
templated the way their ancient march still speaks to us.
There were very good reasons for everything God commanded the children of Israel to do in preparation for their
entrance into the Promised Land. The ceremonial cleansing
tells us, symbolically, that we must not presume upon God's
goodness. True, we are cleansed from all sin at the moment
of our salvation (Red Sea crossing), but an intimate
Christian walk requires a daily cleansing—an abiding in the
blood of Jesus.

On the day of the crossing of the Jordan, everyone was to focus upon the ark of God. This ark was the vessel through which God communicated to His people and where He manifested His glory. It also represented the coming Messiah who would be a living revelation of God's glory. Jesus Christ, the Messiah, is the One to whom we look under the New Covenant to guide us into the promised land.

As with the Israelites, we cannot see the glory of God until we have been cleansed, first at our "Red Sea" salvation experience and, later, in preparation for crossing our "Jordan." Only then can we hope to see the miracle of God. Once we see the ark—Jesus—our eyes are never to lose sight of Him. We should be so submitted to and identified with the Lord that we no longer consider ourselves individuals headed on separate paths. Instead, we recognize our oneness and long to fulfill our function in this vast body, following the guidance of its Head. When God says to move, we must move—not before and not later, but then.

What must have passed through the minds of the priests and Levites as they paused on the bank of the Jordan with several million people behind them? Whatever doubts may have assailed them in that instant before their feet touched the water was not enough to deter them from their course of action. God had spoken, and that settled it for them. They stepped out boldly on the Word of God. And oh, how their faith was rewarded!

The mighty power of the living God rolled the waters back. Think of the awesome joy the people must have experienced as they passed those loyal leaders. Every Israelite filed past the spot where the priests and Levites stood holding the ark, and each one knew that God—their God—was real. Our God has not changed. He still rewards faithful obedience with miracles.

While the people crossed the river, the Lord commanded that twelve stones, one for each tribe, should be brought from the place where the priests stood in the middle of the once-raging waters. These were to be a memorial to God's glory forever.

> When your children ask their fathers in time to come, saying, "What are these stones?" then you shall inform your children, saying, "Israel crossed this Jordan on dry ground." For the LORD your God dried up the waters of the Jordan before you until you had crossed, just as the LORD your God had done to the Red Sea, which He dried up before us until we had crossed; that all the peoples of the earth may know that the hand of the LORD is mighty, so that you may fear the LORD your God forever.
> —JOSHUA 4:21–24, NAS

Years later, another memorial would be built, but with less fruitful results. The two and one-half tribes of Reuben, Gad and Manasseh who chose not to remain in the Promised Land, but to return to the east side of the Jordan, built a monument there in the shape of an altar. Already, because of their separation from the rest of Israel, confusion set in. The intentions of the eastern tribes were good, but how they were misunderstood by the rest of the Israelites! "And when the sons of Israel heard of it, the whole congregation of the sons of Israel gathered themselves at Shiloh, to go up against them in war" (Joshua 22:12).

So great was the confusion that the remaining tribes thought the two and one-half tribes were committing idolatry and should be put to death. What actually occurred there on the east bank of the Jordan? What motivated them to build a second altar? Their intention was not to worship another god besides Jehovah. Rather, they desired to maintain a semblance of unity with the other tribes. The priests learned the truth by coming to speak with the supposed idolaters. The eastern tribes recognized that the Jordan River would forever separate them physically from the rest of the tribes, and they did not want to lose their identity as God's people.

> Therefore we said, "Let us now prepare to build ourselves an altar, not for burnt offering nor for sacrifice, but that it may be a witness between you and us and our generations after us, that we may perform the service of the LORD before Him with our burnt offerings, with our sacrifices, and with our peace offerings; that your descendants may not say to our descendants in time to come, 'You have no part in the LORD.'"
> —JOSHUA 22:26–27

With the decision to separate from the rest of the tribes, the strong unity of the children of Israel was destroyed. This division greatly hurt those smaller tribes of Reuben and Gad and the half-tribe of Manasseh. Any time the Israelites' enemies attacked them from the east, it was the two and one-half tribes who suffered the brunt of the attack—all because they were not united with the rest of their brothers.

As we studied earlier, our strength lies in the unity of the body of Christ. I know in my own life that when I do not choose to maintain spiritual oneness with other believers, I place myself in a position of vulnerability to attack from the enemy. Also, we must always remember that we serve the one true God. Abraham described Him as the Creator of all people, and His love goes past every denominational barrier.

Another lesson concerns attitude. We should be careful not to become unnecessarily suspicious of other believers. We are all individuals and will express our worship differently, but that is no reason to cast a wary eye at someone else. The Word is our ultimate judge. We may be hesitant about what we think someone else believes, when in truth, they are totally and intimately in love with the Lord.

Imagining what another believer thinks can often cause serious strife and gaps between Christians. Essentially, people who love the Lord with all their heart, mind and soul will think alike. God, who lives within them, transforms all His children into the image of His Son, Jesus. In Colossians 2:2, Paul encourages true intimacy with the Lord and each other.

> [For my concern is] that their hearts may be braced (comforted, cheered and encouraged) as they are knit together in love, that they may come to have all the abounding wealth and blessings of assured conviction and understanding, and that they may become progressively more intimately acquainted with, and may know more definitely and accurately and thoroughly, that mystic secret of God, [which is] Christ, the Anointed One.
>
> —COLOSSIANS 2:2, AMP

God is calling us to identify completely with Christ, to enter into an intimate relationship with Him and His people in Canaan. Our minds need to be attuned to His thoughts. Whatever good we do, we must realize that it is God's Spirit who has sanctioned it and is performing the act through us. We must see ourselves, not as solitary individuals, but as important and cherished members of Christ's body. We are sons of God…children of the King.

Whenever God directs us to begin a new walk of faith, there may be times when the majority will not side with us. (This is not to be confused with the division caused by the two and one-half tribes.) Consider Joshua and Caleb. They were outnumbered ten to two among the spies. Democracy is not always correct or practical, especially concerning matters of the Spirit. However, we can be assured of making the proper decisions if we abide in Christ and do not rebel against His leadership by refusing the guidance of the Holy Spirit.

Faith marches forth courageously in God's strength and does not see itself as a grasshopper confronting Canaanite giants. If only the Israelites had trusted and acted on the direction of the Holy Spirit they would have entered the Promised Land in one-thirtieth of the time. This is something for us to keep in mind, both in work and in our personal lives. I know there are times when, faced with large tasks, I fall prey to the grasshopper syndrome. The answer lies in becoming *intimate* with God. Courage like that of Joshua and Caleb grows out of a deep and abiding knowledge of God's all-encompassing love. He will never fail us!

Not long ago we found it necessary to build a new facility to more easily and economically accommodate the number of patients coming to St. Luke's. To all appearances this project seemed impossible. However, through much prayer and careful planning, God was true to His namesake. He was, and is, Jehovah-Jireh—the Lord our provider. A seventy-eight thousand square-foot clinic housing six operating suites was built in ten months. One year after the plans were made we moved into the newly certified building!

Whatever activities we personally engage in, whether looking in a microscope or pushing a broom, we need to see ourselves as God sees us. He sent His Son to die for us that we might know Him—each one who will answer His call, "Come unto Me." I ask the people I work closely with to identify themselves not as Tom, Dick, Mary or Jane, but as God's children. In this way we can work together without pride, greed, envy or the like interfering. When we see through the Father's eyes and begin to understand how precious each life is, how can our faith and belief help but to grow, and our deeds become bolder?

At some point, like Joshua and Caleb, each of us will face the decision to cross the Jordan with the Lord. He is the only One capable of assuaging the hindering currents, turning them into solid ground beneath our feet. Our faith, like theirs, must be real and our actions strong.

Canaan at last! The land of milk and honey. A land of beauty and plenty (symbolic of an intimate relationship with God)—filled with giants and unfriendly natives. The Lord gave specific and absolute commands how the Israelites should deal with them.

> And when the LORD your God shall deliver them before you, and you shall defeat them, then you shall utterly destroy them. You shall make no covenant with them and show no favor to them. Furthermore, you shall not intermarry with them; you shall not give your daughters to their sons, nor shall you take their daughters for your sons. For they will turn your sons away from following Me to serve other gods; then the anger of the LORD will be kindled against you, and He will quickly destroy you.
> —DEUTERONOMY 7:2–4, NAS

Obedience was as necessary for survival in Canaan as in the wilderness. God's instructions were for the Israelites' own protection. He knew that if they failed to destroy the evil completely, it would come back to haunt them. They failed, and it did. Countless times throughout the history of Israel, Scripture tells of battle after battle with those cultures and their descendants.

Just as the Israelites neglected to destroy the evil influences in their new country, so have I sometimes delayed in putting an end to evil in my life. I have begun to walk a submitted life, a life filled with the Holy Spirit, to be equipped to fight in my "Canaan." Failure to obliterate sin prevents us from walking intimately and victoriously with God, from ever becoming true *beatitudinal* Christians.

We have seen how, during the Israelites' journey throughout the wilderness to the Promised Land, God's commitment to His people was divinely unconditional. Even though they rebelled and complained, wandered astray and disobeyed, grew faint and fearful, He remained faithful to them. He was the great Shepherd of Israel and Owner of His sheep. Working through Moses, and later Joshua, as earthly shepherds to whom the people could relate, God led His chosen people home.

The intense devotion of the Divine Shepherd for His sheep inspired the beautiful twenty-third Psalm of King David many years after the Israelites reached Canaan. How descriptive it is of their trek through the wilderness, and of our own:

> The LORD is my shepherd; I shall not want,
> He makes me to lie down in green pastures;
> He leads me beside the still waters.
> He restores my soul;
> He leads me in the paths of righteousness
> For His name's sake.
> Yea, though I walk through the valley of the shadow of death,
> I will fear no evil;
> For You are with me;
> Your rod and Your staff, they comfort me.
> You prepare a table before me in the presence of my enemies;
> You anoint my head with oil;
> My cup runs over.
> Surely goodness and mercy shall follow me

All the days of my life;
And I will dwell in the house of the LORD
Forever.

Like Moses, David understood the unwavering devotion of a shepherd for his sheep. As a young man, he learned how dependent the sheep were upon him for food, water and protection. God chose both Moses and David and prepared them in the wilderness for the enormous responsibility of leadership—as shepherds of His people. Yet, even as great as these men were, they paled in comparison to Jesus, who declared:

> I am the good shepherd. The good shepherd gives His life for the sheep...My sheep hear My voice, and I know them, and they follow Me. And I give them eternal life, and they shall never perish; neither shall anyone snatch them out of My hand.
> —JOHN 10:11, 27–28

Divine covenant. Ultimate commitment. A never-ending love that guarantees eternal protection, from the only One who can deliver on such promises. The Lord our Shepherd, *Jehovah-Rohi*, is calling us to Himself, to trust Him with our whole life. He will feed, clothe, protect us from all evil and lead us to our promised land if we will just follow Him. He gave the gift of the Holy Spirit to indwell every believer, to guide and work through us. He does not want a recurrence of the division and confusion between the tribes living on both sides of the Jordan River.

The dangers of the world lurk a short distance from the flock, a distance as great as that between day and night or between shadow and light. In the shadows lurk the hidden things that would steal from, kill and destroy the people of God. In the light of our Shepherd are protection, health and life.

I am the light of the world. He who follows Me shall
not walk in darkness, but have the light of life.

—JOHN 8:12

How we need the life-giving light that comes from following Jesus! Separated from the rest of the flock, our light
will only grow dim as the wick remains untrimmed and the
oil runs low. It is not individuals, but the body of Christ, His
bride, who will be victorious. When we realize that God is
Light, we will be able to appreciate the need for wilderness
times in our lives in order to become intimate with Him. At
one time, we were all living in darkness, and had darkness
within us. Light can have no fellowship with darkness
(2 Corinthians 6:14); therefore, we could have no union
with our God. Light dispels darkness!

Lovingly submitted to the lordship of Jesus, our lives will
reflect His victory in us. When we listen to the voice of our
Shepherd, the possibility of getting into trouble is slim. When
we do not listen, we take our chances, and our problems are
many. Even as the children of Israel failed to listen to their
Shepherd, I have done the same.

One time during our desert voyage, I ran from Jericho to
an area near Masada without water, compass or companion.
I left Jerusalem at 4:00 A.M. that morning, intending to run
to Qumran where I would meet the buses. I had planned for
it to be one of my long morning runs of twenty to twenty-
five miles. It was long, all right. Over fifty miles long!

Running alone, I got lost in the unfamiliar terrain of the
Judean desert. Soon I was not only dehydrated, but also
scratched and torn from attempting to climb down cave-like
walls near the Dead Sea to the highway beneath where I
could find help. Even in the midst of my mistakes God was
still merciful. Suddenly I spotted an unusual passageway

down the caves to Qumran. Without that serendipity, it is quite likely that I would now be experiencing true intimacy with the Lord—in heaven.

We all need a companion in our "desert," but more than that, we need a Shepherd. Without the guidance of God's Spirit we become hopelessly lost. Pride in our own knowledge of the desert is deadly, for it breeds only spiritual dwarfs stumbling through the shadows. If we are stiff-necked, we cannot operate within His framework of wisdom, knowledge, thought or direction. We will never rise to a strong spiritual level unless we allow ourselves to be conformed to His Spirit.

Most of the Israelites tried to avoid discipline by either God or Moses. We too often choose paths that are easy for us. In the twenty-third Psalm, David noted that the rod and staff of the shepherd *comforted* him. The letter to the Hebrews also emphasizes the loving motives behind God's correction:

> My son, do not regard lightly the discipline of the Lord, nor faint when you are reproved by Him; for those whom the Lord loves He disciplines, and He scourges every son whom He receives…He disciplines us for our good, that we may share His holiness. All discipline for the moment seems not to be joyful, but sorrowful; yet to those who have been trained by it, afterwards it yields the peaceful fruit of righteousness.
>
> —HEBREWS 12:5–6, 10–11, NAS

Discipline yields fruit. We are reminded of Joshua and Caleb, the only two of the original generation of Israelites who allowed God's discipline to strengthen them and who went into the Promised Land to claim the fruit of righteousness found there. Following in their footsteps, we too can conquer the giants who oppose the work of God. It is essential that we commit our bodies as living sacrifices to God—physical discipline is supportive and secondary to spiritual life. Caleb must have been in good condition at the age of eighty-five, enough so to attack the giant Anakims at Hebron. What an example of physical, mental and spiritual strength! Like Joshua who commanded the sun and moon to stand still in the heavens, our lives too can be a visible sign that God still fights for His people.

An intimate union with the Lord in Canaan requires that we submit our entire being—physical, mental and spiritual—to His direction. Without any reservations, we should cultivate the habit of reading the Word, praying and listening intently for His leading. "Pray and obey," the message of Moses and Jesus, is the same word for today given by Dr. David Yonggi Cho, pastor of the world's largest church. He attributes the phenomenal move of God in his country of South Korea to a disciplined adherence to this simple truth.

Many people attempt to become intimate with God but lack a sound biblical foundation. This can lead to involvement with cults utilizing bizarre behavior. Paul warns us to stay steadfast (Colossians 2:5, 7). He urges us to beware of philosophies and legalisms that could destroy our intimacy with God (Colossians 2:4, 8). *Pisteuo* is a Greek word meaning "to believe—to adhere to, to have faith in; to rely on." Thus, to believe in God means to have an intimate, absolute, personal reliance upon the Lord. The verse, "Believe on the Lord Jesus Christ, and you will be saved" (Acts 16:31), takes on an entirely different meaning when seen in this light. Genuine intimacy with God is a result of much time spent with Him—listening, following and obeying His Word (John 15; Exodus 19:4–6; Deuteronomy 28; Joshua 1:8). (For more information on a balanced, intimate Christian walk, you might want to read my book titled, *The Dynamics of Worship*.[1])

The relationship between God and man is no longer limited to laws written on tablets of stone. Scripture states that He now writes His laws in our hearts and minds, transforming us into His likeness (Hebrews 8:10; 10:16). Continued intimacy with God leads to a life filled with the fruit of the Spirit: "love, joy, peace, longsuffering, kindness, goodness, faithfulness, gentleness, self-control" (Galatians 5:22–23). Abundant spiritual fruit in our lives is the outward manifestation of this inner transformation. It is the ability to glorify God in every earthly endeavor. Ultimately, we will be able to love as He loves.

The Lord spoke to Moses face-to-face as a man would speak to his friend (Exodus 33:11). What a privilege! Similarly, our relationship with our heavenly Father through the Holy Spirit must be one of utmost closeness, yet of respect, as a son who is privileged to call his father "Daddy." This relationship should be more real and inspiring than any other in our life. Such intimacy leaves all things unbarred in His presence. Are we ready for a continual face-to-face relationship with Him, or will we be content to remain on the other side of the Jordan like the two and one-half tribes?

CHAPTER 7

Eternity's Call

C ome unto Me...God's heart-cry for intimacy with man, has been echoing for centuries. The Father beckoned His people throughout the wilderness with that message. It is true that a marriage (symbolizing the most sacred and intimate of relationships) did take place in the Sinai when the Lord asked Israel to be His bride, and they accepted His proposal. However, they became backsliders and apostates, and the Lord eventually gave them a certificate of divorce (Isaiah 50:1; Jeremiah 3:8).

With His mercy extending as high as the heavens, the Father promised to come to His people again. We know that He did so through His only Son, the Messiah, Jesus Christ (Matthew 23:37–39). Jesus came to walk among mankind as a man to continue the Father's call and encourage us to Himself:

> Come to Me, all you who labor and are heavy laden, and I will give you rest. Take My yoke upon you and learn from Me, for I am gentle and lowly in heart.
> —MATTHEW 11:28

> If anyone thirsts, let him come to Me and drink.
> —JOHN 7:37

Finally, Jesus sent His Holy Spirit to live within us and sustain the call for greater intimacy with Himself, in preparation for us to be eternally one with the Father. The Holy Spirit is urging us, the bride, to join with Him in praying for Jesus' return, "And the Spirit and the bride say, 'Come!'...He who testifies to these things says, 'Surely I am coming quickly'" (Revelation 22:17, 20).

A bride calling her bridegroom...the bridegroom wooing his long-awaited mate...what could be more tender and intimate? Jesus promised that, as the Bridegroom, *He will return* to claim His virgin bride, the church. We are that bride, even now being made ready to be presented to Him on our wedding day. But will His call continue indefinitely? Jesus taught a startling parable that gives us the answer—the parable of the ten virgins.

> Then the kingdom of heaven will be comparable to ten virgins, who took their lamps, and went out to meet the bridegroom. And five of them were foolish, and five were prudent. For when the foolish took their lamps, they took no oil with them, but the prudent took oil in flasks along with their lamps. Now while the bridegroom was delaying, they all got drowsy and began to sleep. But at midnight there was a shout, "Behold, the bridegroom! Come out to meet him." Then all those virgins rose and trimmed their lamps. And the foolish said to the prudent, "Give us some of your oil, for our lamps are going out." But the prudent answered, saying, "No, there will not be enough for us and you too; go instead to the dealers and buy some for yourselves." And while they were going away to make the purchase, the bridegroom came, and those who were ready went in with him to the wedding feast; and the door was shut. And later the other virgins also came, saying, "Lord, lord, open

up for us." But he answered and said, "Truly I say to you, I do not know you." Be on the alert then, for you do not know the day nor the hour.

—MATTHEW 25:1–13, NAS

The truth is, the moment will soon be upon us when God's plea for intimacy with man will cease. Though our Bridegroom is tarrying, He will return suddenly. "I will come upon you as a thief, and you will not know what hour I will come upon you" (Revelation 3:3). We have seen how every other promise God made to His people through the ages He has fulfilled. Surely, He will consummate this one also. Are we prepared to meet Him? Our garments—how clean are they? Are they without spot or wrinkle, washed in the blood of the Lamb? (See Ephesians 5:27.) A marriage celebration awaits us...

> Let us be glad and rejoice and give Him glory, for the marriage of the Lamb has come, and His wife has made herself ready. And to her it was granted to be arrayed in fine linen, clean and bright, for the fine linen is the righteous acts of the saints. Then He said to me, "Write: 'Blessed are those who are called to the marriage supper of the Lamb!'" And He said to me, "These are the true sayings of God."
>
> —REVELATION 19:7–9

Hallelujah! A magnificent wedding feast is being prepared for us in heaven. In that final hour on earth, the Bridegroom will call His bride one last time, no longer with gentle, wooing words of, "Come unto me..." but with the herald trumpet of angels:

> But immediately after the tribulation of those days the sun will be darkened, and the moon will not give its light, and the stars will fall from the sky, and the powers of the heavens will be shaken, and then the

sign of the Son of Man will appear in the sky, and
then all the tribes of the earth will mourn, and they
will see the Son of Man coming on the clouds of the
sky with power and great glory. And He will send
forth His angels with a great trumpet and they will
gather together His elect from the four winds, from
one end of the sky to the other...and the dead in
Christ shall rise first. Then we who are alive and
remain shall be caught up together with them in the
clouds to meet the Lord in the air, and thus we shall
always be with the Lord.

—MATTHEW 24:29–31;
1 THESSALONIANS 4:16-17, NAS

Amen and amen...so be it!

Epilogue

As the midday heat pounded down on Mount Sinai, the time arrived for our group of twelve desert voyagers to leave for home. I realized more than ever that all the happenings of the Sinai were a showcase of God's miraculous relationship with man, now and for eternity. Although my life had followed the gritty path of Moses and the Israelites in the wilderness, the intimacy and love God offered overshadowed my sin and opened the way for true obedience. The selfish side of me would have to begin the metamorphosis to agape love before I could ever enter Canaan, the promised land of God. Walking down the mountain, I wondered if I could keep the commitment to God's will, as did Joshua and Caleb. One thing was certain. In my own strength, it was, and still is, impossible. Abiding in Jesus, *all* things are possible. The choice is mine.

In these pages you have read of God's love, of His desire for our fellowship and of the price He paid to endow us with that opportunity. God gave His all for a people who would take joy in His presence. For three and one-half years, the Light blazed brilliantly: blind eyes saw His face; deaf ears heard His words and the dead awoke to see the Man, Jesus. The call of the ages to come unto Him continues, but not forever.

Not one of us could ever earn eternal life. None is worthy, then or now, for "all have sinned and fall short of the glory of God" (Romans 3:23). The natural end result of that sin is death. (See Romans 6:23.) Yet, Jesus Christ came to earth that we might have more abundant life. (See John 10:10.) All we need do is admit our need—that on our own we are not worthy. By His death and glorious resurrection Jesus destroyed Satan's authority and broke the power of sin.

There is only one way that leads to life, one door that opens to this way and one name under heaven by which we may be saved (Acts 4:12). Jesus Christ is the way, the truth and the life. No one can come to the Father except through Him (John 14:6). What then, must you do to be saved? Two thousand years ago, the apostle Paul answered this very question. He said, "Believe on the Lord Jesus Christ, and you will be saved, you and your household" (Acts 16:31). To the Roman church he wrote:

> If you confess with your mouth Jesus as Lord, and believe in your heart that God raised Him from the dead, you shall be saved; for with the heart man believes, resulting in righteousness, and with the mouth he confesses, resulting in salvation.
> —ROMANS 10:9–10, NAS

It is as simple as that. Open your heart and mind up to Jesus. Ask Him to forgive you and to come into your life. Believe that He loves you, that He dwells in you and that you are now forgiven. Let Him fill you with His Holy Spirit. Give thanks that you have been led out of Egypt and are beginning your own walk to the promised land. Tell someone you love of your decision to respond to God's eternal call. You have come unto Him at last. Rejoice!

NOTES

CHAPTER 1

By Divine Appointment

1. Jill Briscoe, *Here Am I; Send Aaron!* (Wheaton, IL: Chariot Victor Books, 1984).

CHAPTER 3

Learning a New Walk

1. Francis Brown, S. Driver, Charles Briggs, *Brown-Driver-Briggs Hebrew and English Lexicon* (Peabody, MA: Hendrickson Publishers, Inc., 1996).

CHAPTER 6

Onward to Victory

1. James P. Gills, M.D., *The Dynamics of Worship* (Tarpon Springs, FL: Love Press, 2002).

Did You Enjoy This Book?

Dr. and Mrs. James P. Gills would love to hear from you! Please let them know if *Come Unto Me* has had an effect in your life or in the lives of your loved ones. Send your letters to:

St. Luke's Cataract and Laser Institute
P.O. Box 5000
Tarpon Springs, FL 34688-5000
Telephone: (727) 938-2020, Ext. 2200
              (800) 282-9905, Ext. 2200
Fax: (727) 372-3605

J ames P. Gills, M.D., is founder and director of St. Luke's
Cataract and Laser Institute in Tarpon Springs, Florida.
Internationally respected as a cataract surgeon, Dr. Gills
has performed more cataract extractions with lens implanta-
tions than anyone else in the world. He has pioneered many
advancements in the field of ophthalmology to make
cataract surgery safer and easier.

As a world-renowned ophthalmologist, Dr. Gills has
received innumerable medical and educational awards, high-
lighted by 1994–1999 listings in *The Best Doctors in America*.
Dr. Gills is a clinical professor of ophthalmology at the
University of South Florida, and was named one of the Best
Ophthalmologists in America in 1996 by ophthalmic aca-
demic leaders nationwide. He serves on the board of direc-
tors of the American College of Eye Surgeons, the Board of
Visitors at Duke University Medical Center, and the
Advisory Board of Wilmer Ophthalmological Institute at
Johns Hopkins University. He has published more than 170
medical papers and authored eight medical textbooks. Listed
in *Marquis Who's Who in America*, Dr. Gills was Entrepreneur
of the Year 1990 for the State of Florida, received the Tampa
Bay Business Hall of Fame Award in 1993, and the Tampa
Bay Ethics Award from the University of Tampa in 1995. In
1996 he was awarded the prestigious Innovators Award by
his colleagues in the American Society of Cataract and
Refractive Surgeons. In 2000 he was presented with the
Florida Enterprise Medal by the Merchants Association of
Florida, named Humanitarian of the Year by the Golda
Meir/Kent Jewish Center in Clearwater, and Free Enterpriser
of the Year by the Florida Council on Economic Education.
In 2001 The Salvation Army presented to Dr. Gills their

prestigious "Others" Award in honor of his lifelong commitment to service and caring.

Dr. Gills has dedicated his life to restoring much more than physical vision. He seeks to encourage and comfort the patients who come to St. Luke's. It was through sharing his insights with patients that he initially began writing on Christian topics. An avid student of the Bible for many years, he now has authored fifteen books dealing with Christian principles and physical fitness.

As an ultra-distance athlete, Dr. Gills participated in forty-six marathons, including eighteen Boston Marathons, and fourteen 100-mile mountain runs. In addition, he completed five Ironman Triathlons in Hawaii and six Double Iron Triathlons. Dr. Gills has served on the national Board of Directors of the Fellowship of Christian Athletes and in 1991 was the first recipient of their Tom Landry Award.

Married in 1962, Dr. Gills and his wife, Heather, have raised two children, Shea and Pit. Shea Gills Grundy, a former attorney now full-time mom, is a graduate of Vanderbilt University and Emory University Law School. She and husband, Shane Grundy, M.D., presented the Gills with their first grandchildren—twins, Maggie and Braddock, and three years later a third child, James Gills Grundy. The Gills' son, J. Pit Gills, M.D., ophthalmologist, received his medical degree from Duke University Medical Center and in 2001 joined the St. Luke's staff. "Dr. Pit" is married to Joy Parker-Gills. They are proud parents of Pitzer and Parker.

OTHER BOOKS BY JAMES P. GILLS, M.D.

RX FOR WORRY: A THANKFUL HEART
Discusses how each of us can find peace by resting and relaxing in the promises of God.
ISBN 0-88419-932-0

LOVE: FULFILLING THE ULTIMATE QUEST
A quick refresher course on the meaning and method of God's great gift.
ISBN 0-88419-933-9

A BIBLICAL ECONOMICS MANIFESTO
(with Ronald H. Nash, Ph.D.)
How the best understanding of economics conforms with what the Bible teaches on the subject.
ISBN 0-88419-871-5

THE PRAYERFUL SPIRIT: PASSION FOR GOD, COMPASSION FOR PEOPLE
Tells how prayer has changed Dr. Gills' life, the lives of patients and other doctors.
ISBN 1-59185-215-3

DARWINISM UNDER THE MICROSCOPE: HOW RECENT SCIENTIFIC EVIDENCE POINTS TO DIVINE DESIGN
Lays a scientific foundation for "divine design" and equips the reader to discuss the topic intelligently.
ISBN 0-88419-925-8

THE UNSEEN ESSENTIAL: A STORY FOR OUR TROUBLED TIMES
A compelling, contemporary novel about one man's struggle to grow into God's kind of love.
ISBN 1-879938-05-7

TENDER JOURNEY: A CONTINUING STORY FOR OUR TROUBLED TIMES
The sequel to The Unseen Essential.
ISBN 1-8779938-17-0

TRANSFORM YOUR MARRIAGE
An elegant 4- by 8.5-inch booklet to help couples develop new closeness with each other and with the Lord.
ISBN 1-879938-11-1

TEMPLE MAINTENANCE: EXCELLENCE WITH LOVE
A how-to book for achieving lifelong total fitness of body, mind and spirit.
ISBN 1-879938-01-4

THE DYNAMICS OF WORSHIP
Designed to rekindle the heart with a passionate love for God. Gives the who, what, when, where, why and how of worship.
ISBN 1-879938-03-0

BELIEVE AND REJOICE: CHANGED BY FAITH, FILLED WITH JOY
How faith in God can let us see His heart of joy.
ISBN 1-879938-13-8

IMAGINATIONS: MORE THAN YOU THINK
How focusing our thoughts will help us grow closer to God.
ISBN 1-879938-18-9